Remembering the Armed Struggle

my time with the red army faction

Margrit Schiller

PMPRESS

KER
SPL
EBE
DEB

2021

First published in German by Konkret-Verlag in 1999
Original translation by Lindsay Munro,
edited by Kersplebedeb for this edition

This edition copyright PM Press and Kersplebedeb, 2021

ISBN: 9781629638737

Library of Congress Control Number: 2020947290

Cover by John Yates / www.stealworks.com

10 9 8 7 6 5 4 3 2 1

PM Press
P.O. Box 23912
Oakland, CA 94623
www.pmpress.org

Kersplebedeb Publishing and Distribution
CP 63560
CCCP Van Horne
Montreal, Quebec
Canada H3W 3H8
www.kersplebedeb.com
www.leftwingbooks.net

Printed in the USA

For Benita and Nicolas

Contents

Acronym Key

BfV: Bundesamt für Verfassungsschutz (Federal Office for the Protection of the Constitution); there is a federal BfV, and each Land also has its own BfV

BKA: Bundeskriminalamt (Federal Criminal Police Office)

BND: Bundesnachrichtendiesnt (Federal Intelligence Service)

CDU: Christlich Demokratische Union Deutschlands (Christian Democratic Union)

GSG-9: Grenzschutzgruppe 9 (Border Protection Group 9)

LKA: Landeskriminalamt (State Criminal Police Office)

MAD: Militärischer Abschirmdienst (Military Counterintelligence Service)

SDS: Sozialistischer Deutscher Studentenbund (Socialist German Student Union)

SPK: Sozialistisches Patientenkollektiv (Socialist Patients' Collective)

RZ: Revolutionäre Zellen (Revolutionary Cells)

Foreword by Ann Hansen

In the early 1980s, I was part of an anarchist-inspired urban guerrilla group in Canada, known as Direct Action. After our capture and a lengthy trial, I was given a life sentence for my part in our campaign of sabotage. I subsequently spent about seven years in the women's federal prison system in the 1980s and early 1990s, as well as a few short parole suspensions in the twenty-first century.

Based on my experiences, I believe the quality that makes Margrit Schiller's memoir so unique is the honesty of her first-hand account, or as people in the 1970s would have said, her ability "to tell it like it is."

Remembering the Armed Struggle documents seven years of Schiller's life in the 1970s, first in the underground, and then in the prisons of West Germany, as a member of the Red Army Faction, one of the most influential urban guerrilla groups of the twentieth century. In retrospect, I can attribute some of my inspiration at the time of Direct Action to the Red Army Faction, even though I had become disillusioned with their Marxist-Leninist ideology by that point.

Schiller recounts how she first encountered the RAF as a political activist in the Socialist Patients' Collective, a radical psychiatry collective. She was unwittingly introduced to the group's founding members when a friend asked if they could use her apartment as a safehouse. Schiller agreed, although she only knew her new roommates by their aliases and before they had begun carrying out public actions.

The narrative unfolds through the prism of Schiller's personal experiences, providing a nuanced picture of the RAF. This rare balance rests on the strength of Schiller's ability to recount stories as she experienced them at the time; she recalls RAF members laughing at jokes in comic books and listening to rock music in her apartment safehouse, just like anyone else. She describes her experiences in a familiar, non-dogmatic style that reflects the fact she was not influenced by preconceived notions about glorified heroes, nor by the vilified urban guerrilla stereotypes portrayed by the mass media.

It is difficult in today's world to imagine the degree of support there once was for urban guerrilla warfare. But the 1960s and 1970s was a time of national liberation movements, often spearheaded by guerrilla fronts that had successfully brought imperialism to its knees: the Chinese Revolution under the guidance of Mao, the Cuban Revolution led by Castro and Che, and the Algerian Revolution, in which Frantz Fanon's groundbreaking book *The Wretched of the Earth* advocated for armed anti-colonial struggle as both therapeutic and effective for a colonized people.

In today's world, even those who support armed struggle in theory may question its value in the absence of a popular revolutionary movement. However, in the 1960s and 1970s, revolutionary collectives, lifestyles, and culture contributed to popular revolutionary movements, even in the heart of the imperialist metropoles. There was no lack of water in which the proverbial fish could swim: the American Indian Movement, the Weather Underground, and the Black Liberation Army in the United States, ETA in Spain, the Red Brigades in Italy, the IRA in Ireland, the FLQ in Quebec, and in West Germany, the Red Army Faction and 2nd of June Movement.

Schiller's memoir not only takes place in a historical period of popular resistance to global imperialism, it also unfolds during a time of growing feminist awareness of patriarchal dynamics, not only in the "straight world" of their parents and society at large, but even among their comrades.

Schiller's critique of the leadership style of Andreas Baader, one of the RAF's founding members, reflects the experiences of other young female revolutionaries in the Black Panthers and Weather Underground, who were also beginning to incorporate a feminist critique and practice into their movements.

Following her capture, *Remembering the Armed Struggle* documents Schiller's harrowing experiences of almost six years in the isolation and sensory deprivation cells that were the centerpiece of the nascent counterinsurgency prison program in West Germany. It is worth remembering that a number of RAF prisoners would die behind the prison walls, and that the struggles of the political prisoners were often of critical importance to the group. Schiller provides chilling accounts of the groundbreaking psychological torture techniques used to destroy political prisoners: solitary confinement and sensory deprivation, isolated yard time in physical restraints, constant transfers, twenty-four-hour-a day florescent lighting and surveillance, censorship of mail, and interruption of sleep for count and cell searches.

Indeed, her account of her years in West Germany's prison system is like looking through a porthole into the future. In the 1970s, the left was shocked as the West German state unrolled increasingly repressive legislation and prison conditions aimed not only at isolating the political prisoners but at literally destroying them when they dared to resist. Unfortunately, by the twenty-first century, the left has become numb to the slow creep of the same repressive legislation and prison conditions that were once directed solely at political prisoners, but which have now become normalized, targeting any prisoner who refuses to submit.

Schiller and the other political prisoners in West Germany were kept in isolation and sensory deprivation conditions, the extreme form being known as the "Dead Wing." Today, there is one prison in the United States that is a stand-alone isolation prison, ADX Florence, in Colorado, but there are at least fifty-seven stand-alone isolation units in prisons across the country. Sainte-Anne-des-Plaines in Quebec is the only stand-alone isolation prison in Canada, but, as in the US, there are many stand-alone isolation units in prisons across this country. In these stand-alone prisons or units, prisoners are held in isolation, often for years at a time, with only one hour of exercise daily and no access to programs of any kind. They are also subjected to 24/7 audiovisual surveillance. The administrative decision to keep prisoners isolated is often not related to their sentences or charges but, rather, to their behavior in the prison, their status as so-called "gang members," or their involvement in "radical movements." Some of these prisoners could be labelled "political prisoners"; a disproportionate number are dealing with mental health issues, are racialized, and are being punished for allegedly posing "a threat to the good order of the institution."

Schiller describes "special units" where political prisoners were isolated in small groups. In Canada, almost half the women sentenced for murder are convicted for murdering an abusive partner or acquaintance whom they had previously reported to the authorities. These women must spend a minimum of two years in a maximum security unit where they are segregated from all other prisoners with the exception of the five women in their "pod." The women in these "pods" are subjected to intensive 24/7 audiovisual surveillance. There is usually no work and only one hour of daily exercise in a yard the size of a tennis court. These conditions predictably produce paranoia and anxiety, and they are not targeting political prisoners but everyday people.

Schiller recounts brainwashing techniques used to destroy the identity of the political prisoners. In today's Canadian women's prisons, the maximum security units use "dialectical behavior therapy," or DBT, as their "dynamic security model." Participation in DBT is theoretically voluntary, but if a woman's Correctional Plan stipulates participation in DBT and she chooses not to, there is a high likelihood that she will not be transferred out of the maximum security unit until she complies. In other words, it's the kind of offer you can't refuse.

As such, it is horrific to observe how various techniques that Schiller recounts as having been pioneered against political prisoners in West Germany have become ubiquitous in the twenty-first century.

Margrit Schiller's memoir shows us that the future is now.

Acknowledgements

I would like to thank Barbara Hillecke and Helga and Jutta Windeck for their patient support and constructive criticism. I thank Cuba and my Cuban friends, especially Teresa Prado who helped me find my path toward writing. I would also like to thank Thomas Gruenewald and Karen Francia, our chosen family in Uruguay—visiting them is still always a treat for my children—and Hilary Sandison, who gave me the courage to go on writing when everything seemed so futile. Without the help of Ernesto Kroch and Eva Weil the manuscript for this book would still be lying in my desk drawer. And I would like to say sorry to all of those who I left behind in my life without explanation, first and foremost Helma Beierlein and Gabi.

I believe that in our struggle we have assumed a personal responsibility that we have to commit to in our own names. In most cases, I use the real names of those who are either well-known or dead. The unknown or those who have remained incognito should remain so: Bernd, Christiane, Christina, Ingrid, and Stefan are imaginary names for non-imaginary people.

Remembering the Armed Struggle

Arrest in Hamburg

October 21, 1971. I had spent the previous four weeks, night and day, hiding in a Hamburg apartment from the police. On September 25, there had been a shootout with the police at a train station carpark in Freiburg. I was there but hadn't been one of the shooters. Despite the arrest warrant with my name on it, I had managed with a great deal of effort to get to Hamburg, where I was now living underground.

On this October 21, a meeting with some RAF members had been arranged at another apartment in Hamburg. In addition to some political questions and our next campaign, I was also on the agenda. I didn't know if I still wanted to stay with the RAF, but did I have a choice?

For the RAF, Hamburg had become a dangerous place. Astrid Proll had been arrested in Hamburg in May, and Petra Schelm had been killed there in July in an exchange of gunfire with the police, during which Werner Hoppe was arrested. The same fate could be waiting for any one of us. And since the shootout in Freiburg, the police were also looking everywhere for me.

Attending the meeting meant leaving my hiding place for the first time since arriving in Hamburg. To avoid being recognized, I had cut my reddish-brown hair short and dyed it black. I put on a red minidress and over that a knee-length black coat. I almost felt like I was in fancy dress. The police description said that I generally wore pants. I put on make-up to cover up my high cheekbones and make my eyes look different.

I kept a pistol I had recently been given in my handbag. I had never shot a gun in my life, but with the police looking for me I did not feel safe, and the gun gave me a feeling of security. But I hoped I wouldn't have to use it.

We had decided to set off for the meeting during the early evening rush hour so that there would be less chance of someone recognizing us. It was already dark when the three of us made our way to the apartment where the meeting was to take place next. We took detours, changed subways and commuter trains several times, and were careful to observe what went on around us to make sure we weren't being followed. We separated at the Alstertal commuter train station, each of us taking a separate route to the apartment on this last leg of our journey through the city.

Ulrike Meinhof, Jan-Carl Raspe, Irmgard Möller, Manfred Grashof, Holger Meins, Klaus Jünschke, and three or four others turned up at the apartment one by one. Whether Gudrun Ensslin or Andreas Baader came later or stayed in West Berlin that night, I can't remember.

The apartment looked like all RAF dwellings: a few foam mattresses with bed covers strewn around the floor, a telephone, two radios, a few suitcases and bags, tools, weapons, ammunition, explosives. The windows were covered with lengths of cloth with slits cut in them so we could watch the street outside.

Once in the apartment, all weapons were laid aside, and I put my handbag against one of the walls. Everyone took a good look at my new outfit. One of the radios was tuned in to the police frequency, and one of us was closely following what was being said there at all times. Whenever something happened on the radio that seemed relevant, the others moved in closer to hear exactly what was going on. The plan was that we all stay overnight and then leave the apartment one by one the following day.

It was already after midnight when Holger, who I hadn't seen for weeks, asked me what had happened during the shootout in Freiburg. I had just begun to explain when he interrupted me and asked in an aggressive tone: "So why didn't you shoot?" I caught my breath; I was completely taken aback, became red in the face, and didn't answer. It was a question nobody had asked me before then, one I hadn't even asked myself to be honest. If truth be told, in my opinion, the comrade with me had overreacted and shot too hastily. I still didn't answer. The question about why I hadn't shot was gnawing at me, and it stayed with me even after Holger started to talk about plans for a bank robbery.

Then Ulrike came in: "I have to use the phone. You, come with me," she said to Gerhard Müller. Looking around the room to see who else should come along, she pointed to me: "Come on, you too." Ulrike had spent most of her life in Hamburg and was well-known there, so she was always very nervous in the city. There was a telephone in the apartment, but we never called from one apartment to another. We were sure the telephones were often being tapped, which is why Ulrike wanted to go to a payphone.

The three of us left the apartment, separating at the front door: Ulrike proceeded alone, while Gerhard and I followed at a distance, keeping her in sight. The apartment block was L-shaped and faced a shopping mall with two large car parks leading to Heegbarg Street.

Ulrike crossed Heegbarg, and we walked along the side of the car park in the same direction as her. When we reached the second car park, Gerhard said under his breath: "Watch out for that Ford over there with the dimmed lights! There are two guys sitting in it, and they're probably pigs." Ulrike seemed to have noticed the light-colored car, because she disappeared behind some bushes in front of a low building. We continued walking.

After what seemed like a long time but was probably only a couple of minutes, Ulrike came out onto the sidewalk at the other end of the building, and we immediately crossed the road to be closer to her. The light-colored Ford moved forward—the lights now on full—and slowly exited the car park. At the first intersection, Ulrike turned left onto Saseler Damm and crossed the road diagonally, while we stayed back waiting for the light to change to green. Then we continued walking, no longer behind Ulrike but straight along Heegbarg. The Ford, the only car to be seen anywhere, didn't follow us but turned onto Saseler Damm.

All of a sudden things got loud. We heard footsteps running and tires screeching. We stayed where we were, but when we turned around Ulrike was bolting toward us. "Shit, it's the pigs!" she shouted. Right then, the Ford rounded the corner at high speed, driving past Ulrike trying to block her path by pulling up onto the sidewalk. The passenger door burst open and a man in civilian clothes jumped out. "Stop!" he screamed, "Don't move! Police!" Ulrike was faster, and she managed to get around the car, shouting to us, "Quick, get out of here!" while running like hell down Heegbarg. Gerhard followed right away, quickly catching up with her, and both of them fled along a pathway adjacent to a row of houses. One of the policemen followed, while I remained frozen in place, just watching what was happening.

The policeman caught up to Ulrike and managed to get hold of her handbag. She stumbled but then tore herself free. Gerhard, who was now running in front of Ulrike, stopped, turned around with his weapon drawn, and fired. Once, twice, again and again. The policeman fell, and his colleague, who had followed the three of them, threw himself to the ground. I heard more shots, and then Ulrike and Gerhard disappeared into the darkness.

I had watched the scene unfold before me and couldn't believe my eyes. It was the very same situation I had been in four weeks ago at the shootout in Freiburg.

When everything had quietened down, I regained my senses. I saw the plainclothes policemen's car sitting empty: the doors were wide open, and I could hear the quiet squawking of the police radio. I took a few steps and was next to the car, saw that the key was still in the ignition, got behind the wheel, and drove off. "They can't follow Ulrike and Gerhard without their car," I thought to myself.

It never occurred to me to use the car for my own escape. I parked it on the next dark side street and continued on foot.

I tried desperately to think of what to do next, but my mind was a blank, and my head felt like it was stuck in a vice. Thoughts moved through my head the same way my feet were moving along the sidewalk: slow, halting, unsure. Should I call the others in the nearby apartment and warn them? Would I find the number in the telephone book? Could I even remember the name of the landlord? Could I return to the other apartment where I had been hiding out for weeks? Would I find them?

I had no answers, but it seemed that I should call the apartment. It didn't even occur to me that they would have been listening in to the police radio and would already know something was up. I continued slowly along the street as a police car with flashing blue lights and sirens passed me by. I knew it was all over, that I was going to be arrested.

Unsure of what to do, I went to a payphone. I leafed through the telephone book again and again, picked up the receiver, hung up again. Nothing came to mind—no name, no street, nothing at all.

A car stopped next to the telephone box and a man with a pistol in his hand got out and said, "Police, your documents." When I reached into my handbag to look for my ID, the policeman grabbed the bag from me and discovered the gun.

Then things got intense.

The plainclothes policemen frisked me looking for more weapons. They handcuffed me, pushed me into the back seat of the car, and took me to the nearest police station. I was brought to a room, where two policemen watched over me with their pistols drawn. One of them searched me again, and when I protested he said, "Here, you have absolutely no say whatsoever." Men in plainclothes and in uniform were constantly coming in to have a look at me. "That's her, the one who killed our colleague," they were saying. That was how I learned that the policeman who had almost caught Ulrike was dead, the other slightly injured. A human being was dead. It was something I had known might happen.

After an hour or two, they transferred me to police head-quarters. The hectic to and fro continued there through the night—for the first time in the as yet short history of the RAF, a policeman had been shot. Even though it soon became clear that the shot had not come from my weapon, I was held responsible for the death. The arrest warrant issued against me hours later was for murder and attempted murder.

Shortly after my arrest, because of my height, there was speculation that I had to be the Margrit Schiller they were looking for. I heard them saying that my parents were going to help them identify me, which they did. I wouldn't have expected anything different from them.

The police worked on me for hours, using the murder accusation to shake me up. Who were the other two? Who shot? Where had I come from, and who were my accomplices? "You're a nice, pretty girl; you probably got into the whole thing through a boyfriend. Tell us who the others are, where we can find them, and nothing will happen to you. You'll be out in no time." The longer they talked at me and bombarded me with questions, the calmer and more confident I became. No matter what they did to me, I wouldn't talk. Nothing would make me talk. It occurred to me that I would now be going to prison for ten years, maybe even for life, but I wasn't scared.

My friends in the RAF had often talked about arrest and prison. They told us what they knew about the Tupamaros' experiences in Uruguay, about torture and captivity, about psychological torture and the use of drugs like Pentothal to make prisoners talk. I knew all that, but I still had no idea what an actual arrest would be like or how I would respond to torture. I had no idea what it meant to spend years in prison.

Now that I had been arrested, I felt no fear. While the police ran around frantically throwing questions at me, I sat there—calm and silent. I felt a peace of mind and, at the same time, a sense of heaviness.

What did I have to lose? I didn't have any plans that being arrested would ruin. I didn't feel like I had messed up my life. However, there was a lot to think about: the events of the past weeks had taken me by surprise; I had gotten in over my head. At some point, I had made a step that wasn't right for me, a step that had thrown everything off kilter.

The police had found a fake ID card in my handbag; the only thing on it that was real was my photograph. Now that they knew who I was, they wanted to put me on record: photos, fingerprints, and so on. I realized that that would help them find my last place of residence, and that might help them find my friends, so I decided to do everything I could to prevent them from getting what they wanted. I was starting to feel exhausted after the long stressful night, and I needed a confrontation to stay awake, to draw the battle lines and prepare myself for all that was to come.

Several policemen pulled me roughly to a wash basin. I resisted, and in the scuffle that ensued some tiles were broken. The policemen tried to subdue me, getting me in a stranglehold, tearing at my hair, and pulling at my fingers, which were balled into fists. When they didn't succeed, they got so angry they came close to choking me. Shocked at their own brutality, they backed off.

By this point, I had also had enough, and I stopped resisting. When they photographed me, however, I pulled faces in an attempt to make myself unrecognizable. Although they did manage to take some photos that would be used later during the manhunt, the Hamburg police had devised a plan to get better ones, as I would find out the next day.

Early in the morning, the guards suddenly stepped back. The door opened and a fat, disgusting man came strolling in with what was left of his blonde hair flattened onto his bald head. "Good morning, my name is Rollmann, I'm a member of the Bundestag and a friend of your parents." He said he was a lawyer, and that my parents had asked him to help me. He didn't actually defend terrorists, he added, but because of his friendship with my parents, and so on, and so on. … So my parents had nothing better to do than to dump me with one of their Christian Democrat guys. I cut him off, interrupting his flood of words: "There's no way I'm having my lawyer chosen by my parents. Go to hell!" My harsh tone made it clear that he would get nowhere by continuing to talk, so he snapped his briefcase shut and disappeared.

Over the course of the morning, some strange preparations were being made, making me apprehensive. I was taken by elevator to the top floor of the high-rise police building at Berliner Tor. The policemen surrounding me were tense, and there was a sense of expectation in the air; after about ten minutes they took me down to another floor.

The door to a large room opened right in front of us, and some men with cameras jumped out at me. I went limp and let myself fall, something that the guards on either side of me were not expecting. They got me in a stranglehold and started dragging me by the hair, arms, and legs. I put up a wild struggle, but they hauled me into the large room behind the door where more photographers and cameramen were waiting. The pictures from this "public exhibition" were shown on the TV news that evening and published the following day in all the newspapers.

It was Hamburg Police Chief Günter Redding's plan to serve me up live and without warning to the press so that, with their help, the police could get some good photos for the manhunt. The fact that I had managed to foil their plan boosted my self-confidence.

Because of my resistance, they quickly called off the show, and a police doctor came to see if I had been injured. After that they left me in peace until later that afternoon, when I was taken to the remand prison in Holstenglacis.

I entered the prison building, hands cuffed behind my back and wearing pants and a shirt that were far too small, as my own clothes had been taken from me. An old, high building, a cordon of uniformed male and female guards, a long, dark, green corridor with a lot of heavy doors, then a stairway, and again a corridor with more doors. The head of the women's department, who wore stiletto heels and a colorful, elegant dress, as if she were going to a reception, and heavy make-up, opened a door with one of her many keys, and I entered the cell. The door closed behind me, the key turned, and the lock snapped into place with a loud click. I looked around. Opposite the door was a high window with bars across it. The inside of the window showed how thick the old walls were—it was a bunker. The cell was completely bare apart from a bed, a table, and a chair. There was also a wash basin and a toilet bowl. That was all. I was filled with a great sense of anxiety and exhaustion but also a feeling of calm. So this was where I was going to spend the next days, months, years.

I took a deep breath. It smelled like autumn, and, for the last twenty-five years, I have always been overcome by a profound anxiety whenever I smell the autumn air.

Awakening

In 1966, I was eighteen years old and living in Bonn. Unable to stand life at home any longer, I had left right after finishing my Abitur exams. My father was a major in the German Bundeswehr's Military Counterintelligence Service (Militärischer Abschirmdienst, MAD); all my life he had tried to intimidate and control me with threats and other measures. He always made me feel like he was robbing me of air to breathe. My mother was an adult education teacher and a city councillor in Bonn for the German conservative party, the Christian Democrat Union (Christlich Demokratische Union Deutschlands, CDU).

When I became a teenager, she noticed that I was becoming more and more distant. Both my siblings, Doris, one year younger, and Dieter, two years younger, were still at school when I left home. I had often looked after them on my own when we were children.

My parents were firmly against me moving away and refused to provide any support at all. If I was hungry, they said, I could always come home to eat.

Although I had graduated from high school, I still wasn't sure if I wanted to continue my studies or, if I did, in what subject. Everybody thought it should be math, because I was good at it. But math had too little to do with people for my taste, and studying it seemed to me like living in an ivory tower.

I considered becoming a doctor or a nurse, because I wanted to do something more people-centered. To find out if that was right for me, I went to work at the Johanniter Hospital in Bonn for three months and took a course in assistant nursing. But I found it impossible to meet the patients' needs. Many of them were looking for warmth and affection, grateful for any little gesture of kindness, but the nurses didn't have the time for conversation, and there was nobody else there. The patients were left alone with their worries, and the terminally ill were put in single rooms. When I had time, I often sat by their bedsides to listen and give them the feeling, if only for a few minutes, that they were not alone with their pain. I couldn't maintain a healthy distance between my private life and what I experienced at work, and I even started dreaming about the patients at night.

The hospital hierarchy made me sick. The most important decisions were made by doctors who saw the patients as nothing but numbers on a medical chart, while the nurses never had enough time and were always running around trying to carry out the doctors' orders. In the end, I decided to study psychology.

I rented a room in a student dorm with a friend and enrolled in university. At that time, things were really happening at the University of Bonn psychology department. Heated debates were taking place everywhere you looked about the state of the ossified Federal Republic and where it was heading. Students demonstrated against the Vietnam War, blocking the streets, and young men let their hair grow long, triggering fierce outbursts of anger in the neighborhood where my parents lived. I observed all this going on around me like someone on the outside looking in. Although I sometimes went to meetings and demonstrations, I generally lived the typical student life: working, reading, debating, preparing for exams, listening to rock music, dancing, experimenting with sex. The Kinsey Report, from the United States, the first ever extensive socio-scientific study of human sexuality, was a revelation to me. There was a lot in it that was completely new to me, and it encouraged me to start exploring my own sexuality. For the first time ever, I experienced a feeling of freedom.

I earned my keep by providing nursing care. One woman I attended to several times a week had had a stroke. It had caused amnesia in the part of her brain that controls speech and left her slightly paralyzed on one side. My job was to teach her to speak, read, and write again. She had worked all her life for a large company and proudly showed me the certificates and commendations she had received through-out her career. She had just turned fifty, had no family, and I was the only person who visited. Her life seemed incredibly lonely to me.

Hers was a loneliness I encountered again and again when walking the streets: elderly people talking to themselves or their dog, walking around in their slippers, unkempt. Every time I saw someone like this, it made me sad and angry. Why had these people been left so alone after they retired? Nobody cared about them, because they were no longer of any use to society. I hoped to never end up like that.

At the time, I was looking for new ways to learn, as school had always been torture for me. Every step you took was prescribed by others, and the relationship between teachers and students was cold and hierarchical. Things were very different at university, and I loved it there. The way we lived and studied was no longer regimented, and I could choose what, when, and how I learned and who I discussed things with. I practically devoured the thickest textbooks I could find, and had no problems with learning or concentrating, something that had plagued me throughout my high school years. After only two semesters, I was able to earn money tutoring in statistics.

My mother and I had fierce arguments, because I refused to accept her take on life. She saw that I had rejected her values long before I was even aware of it myself. When I was fifteen, I told her that I didn't want to have children, and that the world would have to change before I changed my mind. She was shocked and begged me never to have an abortion if I got pregnant, saying I should give her the baby instead. That was the last thing I would have done. It was also at fifteen that I took my first small step toward independence by leaving the Church.

My childhood had been oppressive and restrictive, and I left my parents' house with a dull sense of having been maimed in some way. I didn't want to live like my parents or to end up like them. I didn't want "the teachers are always right" or the constant worrying about what the neighbors might think—or the traditional life as a couple and the mandatory nuclear family unit, where thinking or feeling differently was seen as a threat.

I rejected my parents' politics, of course. My mother talked about her party work a lot at home and took us along to CDU meetings. I didn't like the people there, and nothing they were talking about was of interest to me.

When I moved away from home and started taking life into my own hands, I tried to shake off the sadness that had accompanied me for years. Sitting together with friends, we would talk for nights on end about Sartre, Camus, existentialism, and the meaning of life, and I got to know all different kinds of people. I loved the fact that I could go out and meet whoever I wanted whenever I wanted. I studied hard and in the evenings went out with my girlfriend or alone to a local disco, where I would dance like crazy to the music of the Rolling Stones, the Animals, Cream, and Janis Joplin. After I had tired myself out dancing, I would go back to my student room alone.

I was watching television one day and saw the Shah of Iran's secret police beat up protesting university and high school students in West Berlin. It was during this demonstration against the Shah's visit, on June 2, 1967, that a policeman shot and killed the student Benno Ohnesorg.

The whole world was in upheaval, and the existing order was falling apart. In Bolivia, Che Guevara had tried to set up a rural guerrilla force and got killed in the process. In Vietnam, the Viet Cong were organizing resistance "in sandals" against the genocide perpetrated by the United States. The photos of the My Lai massacre in *Stern* magazine shocked me. US soldiers had wiped out an entire village—the women, children, and the elderly—and had then attempted to blame the massacre on the Viet Cong.

Rudi Dutschke came to Bonn and spoke to an audience of thousands about student reforms, the Emergency Laws, the Vietnam War, and rebellion around the world. I went to hear him speak, and the tangible feeling that something new was awakening in society moved me. I was in a process of awakening myself. At this point, I still wasn't interested in the historical facts or the global context of this rebellion, I was more interested in exploring my own personal path in life and trying to find a way to escape being crushed by the constraints of the old order. It was precisely this that made me a part of the movement without me even realizing it. Rudi Dutschke was the best-known spokesperson of the Socialist German Student Union (Sozialistischer Deutscher Studentenbund, SDS), and the newspapers published by the Springer Corporation ranted and raved against him at every opportunity. My father and the other people in his neighborhood shared the anger that could be seen every day back then in the headlines of the *Bild* newspaper: "Demagogues!" "Fifth Column," "Go to the East," "They Just Want to Destroy Everything We Have Created." When Dutschke was seriously injured in April 1968, shot in the head by a far-right sympathizer, I wasn't surprised; it seemed inevitable that the hate against him, against long hair and the new ideas, would end in physical violence.

Even though I felt myself drawn to the student movement, politics were of little interest to me. When Gustav Heinemann became the first member of the Social Democratic Party (Sozialdemokratische Partei Deutschlands, SPD) to be elected federal president, in March 1969, it didn't really mean anything to me, and the Bundestag election in the autumn of 1969 that made Willy Brandt the first SPD chancellor left me cold. Even the passing of the Emergency Laws by the Grand Coalition in 1968 had no impact on me whatsoever. I can remember one heated discussion between my sister and my boyfriend at the time about the Emergency Laws: she was for, he against. It all went over my head; that level of politics was still something abstract and distant for me.

My family had moved to Bonn when I was ten years old, and I had never liked the city, always feeling it to be cramped and full of restrictions and secretive glances. When my boyfriend, who had joined the newly founded German Communist Party (Deutsche Kommunistische Partei, DKP) in the autumn of 1968, became a professor at the University of Mainz and moved there, I used the opportunity to get away. I passed my admissions exams and enrolled at the University of Heidelberg, in April 1970, intending to finish my degree there and be with my boyfriend, whom my parents hated.

I didn't know anyone in Heidelberg. When I arrived, I rented a small basement flat from a friendly family, and would go for long walks along the Neckar River and through the surrounding woodland with my big black dog—a wild mixture of giant schnauzer and hound.

It was difficult to get to know other people and make friends. The years of rebellion in the university, high school, and apprentice movements were over. Things were no longer boiling over, and the debates, which used to spring up spontaneously everywhere you went, and which gave you the opportunity to join in and get to know people, no longer took place. The SDS had been banned in Heidelberg and had fallen apart under the weight of its own contradictions in other cities. The summer of 1970 saw the last big demonstration against state oppression in Heidelberg. The movement was increasingly disintegrating into splinter groups, while the different factions fought fierce battles—generally on paper—against one another with an air of bitter dogmatism. Many of those who, yesterday, had marched through the streets waving the red flag and banners to protest against the Emergency Laws, the Vietnam War, the Shah's murderous regime, or the Springer press's daily attacks, had retreated to concentrating quietly on their studies.

I again felt that keen sense of loneliness that had clung to me in life for as long as I could remember. It seemed to me that this is what life was all about, and that people had no choice but to fight their way through it, alone.

I had read newspaper reports about small groups setting fire to department stores and carrying out bomb attacks in protest against the Vietnam War. However, this was still something very distant from me.

On one occasion, my boyfriend and I drove to Frankfurt to visit his friend Armin Golzem, a lawyer. Like a lot of those on the left at that time, the two of them talked about liberating prisoners and whether or not this was a legitimate part of the fight for a socialist society. In May 1970, force was used to free Andreas Baader, who had been in jail for setting fire to a department store, while he was on a guarded leave from prison. Gudrun Ensslin and Ulrike Meinhof had played an active role in his escape. Armin had met Andreas and Gudrun a year earlier in Frankfurt when they were doing political work with apprentices. My boyfriend and Armin didn't agree with the action to free Andreas, because an uninvolved bystander had been shot and injured during the escape. They both felt that the situation in the Federal Republic was not at a point that justified armed struggle. I listened to them but said nothing. I didn't like the tone they used when they talked about stuff like that—ironic, derisive, aloof. I didn't know it then, but when I would next meet Armin Golzem, two years later, he would be one of my lawyers.

Life as a student, which consisted of reading, studying, and hanging out with my dog and my boyfriend, wasn't really enough for me. I felt that something vital was missing, but I didn't know what. My life needed some kind of meaning. I grew increasingly clear about what it was I didn't want: anything that had to do even remotely with my parents, high school, the area of Bonn I grew up in, or working in a hospital. I didn't want the control, the fear of anything that was different, the barely concealed aggression, or the obsession with order. So I started searching.

At the university, I took note of where and when various groups were meeting from the fliers posted on notice boards. Without knowing anybody, I went to about ten meetings and events organized by different parties and groups—from the Young Democrats to the remnants of the SDS. I generally only went to each group once, because I mostly found the people there boring.

One day in the autumn of 1970, I found a leaflet on the ground that talked about setting up a Release in Heidelberg and that the organizers were looking for people to help them. The idea of the Release was to help drug addicts overcome their heroin addiction by living together with nonaddicts. The Heidelberg Release would be the third such project in West Germany at the time, and the municipal government had provided a vacant building for the project. However, the association had to finance itself, with the goal of becoming an autonomous, independent, self-managed center. I went to the meeting, and I liked the people. There were students, psychologists, a doctor, and a nurse, and they talked openly and directly with one another, making it easy for me to join in.

The building used by the Release was a former printworks, and anybody who wanted to could live there, as long as there was enough space. Everybody cooked together, and the people who lived there slept in groups in the large rooms. The basic day-to-day problems of the residents and the people working there were discussed; for example, how to deal with people who were still secretly shooting up, or whether a handicrafts workshop should be set up to earn money.

Meeting heroin users introduced me to a completely new world. Most of them had grown up in very different circumstances than mine, and many of them had already been to prison. I was very eager to hear other people's stories and learn about their experiences. They had escaped from "normal" life and had become addicted to heroin in their search for something new—and now they were desperately looking for a way out of addiction.

I smoked hash and marijuana for the first time and learned to enjoy music in an entirely new way, much more intensely than before. It was the golden age of rock groups like Deep Purple, Led Zeppelin, and Pink Floyd. However, on the downside, smoking made me feel even more isolated than usual. We went to rock concerts or walked in the woods, listened to Deep Purple at full volume, and smoked. It was nice and terribly lonely at the same time.

I kept my small flat on the banks of the Neckar River but spent most of my time at the Release. We talked all through the night about our lives, our families, our friendships, our sexualities, our plans and dreams for the future. Escaping, living differently, no longer isolated but in a collective, not just working and slaving away but sharing everything, the work and the fun, with one another. Jealousy was caused by possessiveness, and we didn't want possessions. Male structures and male dominance were subjects we talked about over and over again. From one day to the next, I ended the relationship with my boyfriend in Mainz, had several short affairs—one after another and simultaneously—and went to bed with whoever I wanted whenever I wanted. This wasn't without consequences; I contracted gonorrhea more than once. Whenever I went walking along the banks of the Neckar, I would secretively eye the fathers of Heidelberg families and grin to myself, thinking, "If only you knew."

While I lived at the Release, I let others from the center use my flat, for instance, if two of them wanted to spend time alone or if someone was hiding from the police. The Heidelberg police took a hard line against heroin users, who were often beaten up in public and arrested. Drug users who didn't live at the Release were dragged out of their flats along with their belongings, forced onto open-topped trucks with their furniture, and then driven by the police out into the countryside, kilometers away, to be left in the middle of a field with everything they owned. Heidelberg's SPD mayor Rolf Zundel wanted "his" town "junkie-free" at all costs. All of the drug users I met had horror stories to tell about their experiences at the hands of the police.

Their stories reminded me of something I had witnessed in the summer of 1970. I was strolling through town one day when I came across a small group of students who were running away from some helmeted police. I watched as the police tore into the students, who cowered beneath the blows of their batons. I had seen things like this on television, but it was terrible to see it right in front of me. In the face of such brutality, I turned and ran as fast as I could back to the main road, shocked and in tears.

Many of the Release members had taken part in the activities of the APO, the extra-parliamentary opposition, as the protest movements of the late 1960s were known. They told me about street blockades they had organized with high school students the year before to protest against the public transit fare hikes in Heidelberg. When four students were shot dead at Kent State University in the US during a protest against the Vietnam War, it reminded them of their own demonstrations in West Berlin, when they had thrown cobblestones to protest against the ravings of the Springer Corporation and the repression meted out by the courts. But they talked about these things as if they had happened a long time ago; now, they were more interested in their complicated romantic relationships.

It was around this time that I was visited by a friend from Munich. He told me he had set up one of the first communes there, and, as I liked him, I took a few friends to see. The commune consisted of two apartments on two different but connected floors situated in an old tenement building. All they had inside was a few old pieces of furniture, some mattresses, colored fabric on the walls, and a lot of black. Most of the inhabitants had already been thrown out by my friend, who was getting fed up and irritated with the situation. There was very little left of the spirit of awakening.

Goodbye to My Previous Life

After a few weeks of spending most of my time at the Release, I knew there was no future for me there. Heroin had never tempted me, but I looked on as the others, who had joined at the same time as me to help drug users get away from the needle, one by one started shooting up themselves. The idea behind the Release turned back on itself, as those involved started slipping into addiction instead of helping addicts to get out of it.

Some of the friends I had made at the Release were also members of the Socialist Patients' Collective (Sozialistisches Patientenkollektiv, SPK). This was originally a self-help group for doctors and patients who rejected the rigid doctor–patient relationships at the University Hospital of Heidelberg, and who were also opposed to the antiquated university hierarchy. The SPK saw itself as part of a new psychiatry, an "anti-psychiatry."

Well into the 1970s, psychiatric facilities had acted purely as warehouses where the mentally ill were kept quiet with medication and physical restraints. There was no human respect for the ill, nearly all of the treatments involved psychotropic drugs, and electro-shock was used widely.

Anti-psychiatry tried to take the patient and their illness seriously and to find the causes of mental illness within society. Instead of incapacitating and isolating the ill, anti-psychiatry wanted to offer the patient a new social dimension. The movement was inspired by the work of Franco Basaglia in Italy. Basaglia had closed down the large psychiatric institute he was head of, step by step and in cooperation with the doctors and patients. The doctors came down from their pedestal, and the patients were gradually handed back responsibility for their lives in a collective process that involved the entire town.

The SPK considered closed psychiatric units to be an instrument of the state used to exclude and destroy people who lived outside of so-called normality. In contrast to this, the SPK's motto was: "The social system is sick." The basic idea was that illness is a person's reaction to a system that makes them ill, and the solution lies in destroying this system. This idea, which in its simplified notion viewed illness as an important revolutionary force, brought about an extremely fast process of radicalization within the SPK.

The SPK used leaflets and meetings to attack psychiatrists with a Nazi past and to criticize the reactionary politics of the medical and pharmaceutical lobby. The regional government of Baden-Württemberg and its minister-president, the former Nazi navy judge Hans Filbinger (CDU), forced the conflict to a head by banning the SPK from the university.

When I and my friend Gabi, whom I had met at the Release, went to the SPK for the first time in January 1971, everybody knew that their large apartment—which was located in an old tenement block opposite the Heidelberg police headquarters—might be raided and cleared by the police at any time. It was under observation twenty-four hours a day.

The walls of the apartment were covered in slogans, and the large bulletin boards in the hallway were plastered with sheets of paper containing news and information about the subjects and dates of SPK meetings and working groups. Leaflets were produced on an old printing press. Gabi explained what was going on in the SPK and what to expect from the meetings, working groups, and discussions. There was a Marx working group, a Hegel working group, one on anti-psychiatry, and one on the New Left analysis of society. I immediately put my name down for some one-on-one meetings, what the SPK called "individual agitations."

At first, I went to the SPK several times a week for the sole purpose of taking part in these sessions. I felt a great need to talk about myself, my life up to that point, my insecurities, my fears, and my search for something new. During this period, I came to realize that the feelings of loneliness and sadness and many of the problems I had with myself were not my personal fault or some inescapable fate. It was true that my parents, with all their fears, expectations, and disappointments, had pressed me into a "form," but it was possible to break out of this mold. I realized that there were lots of people who felt the same way, and that there were social and political reasons for many of the things people suffered. I understood the Basaglia experiment immediately, because I too had always felt restricted and paralyzed by something that had been a mystery to me previously. This was when I started to get curious about history and politics.

The SPK had books about the Nazi crimes committed during World War II. I read them and was so shocked by what I discovered that I had difficulty sleeping. I remembered a story my father had told my younger sister when she was thirteen and I was fourteen. As so often after work, he had drunk too much, and he was boasting about an incident in Stalingrad where he and some other soldiers had tortured a Russian to death. This was the only time he was open about his "war memories."

Since moving out of my parents' house, I had started remembering and speaking about what had happened at home. But it wasn't until I was in the SPK that I fully realized the sheer brute force with which my parents had suppressed my emotions and my sexuality and how that had made me feel insecure and paralyzed for so many years.

I was nine years old the first time I fell in love with a boy. He was a few years older, and every day after school, pretending I wanted to play with his younger sister, I went to their home and waited longingly to see him. He was all I wanted.

After a while, my mother noticed what was going on, and in an attempt to stifle my feelings forbade me from seeing him again. When that didn't work, she beat me black and blue. First, she sent my younger brother and sister out to play, then she ordered me to undress. She beat me with knitting needles until my back and legs were covered in welts. The next day everybody at school wanted to know what had happened, but I was too ashamed to talk about it. I had actually been an early developer, but this incident set me back so far that I remained childish for years to come.

During puberty, I noticed that my father had strong sexual feelings for me. Although he never physically abused me, I always sensed the way he felt, the intensity of it, and it loomed over me, an omnipresent threat.

It was mostly in bed on Sunday mornings, when I didn't have to get up early to go to school, that I started to explore my own body and dream about sex. It was then that my father would often come into my room, sit down beside me, stroke me, and disturb my intimacy. He often played a game where he pressed himself tightly up against me. He said it was to prove that I couldn't defend myself if a man tried to rape me. For some reason, he found this particularly funny.

As far as he was concerned, I was his possession, and during my entire adolescence he was jealous of every male I had even the slightest contact with. When I was seventeen, he slapped me in the face in front of my first boyfriend and called me a whore. The more my sessions in the SPK made me aware of the connection between my previous inhibitions and the violence at home, especially my father's, the more I felt the need to talk to my parents about it.

I broached the subject the next time I visited them. It took a great deal of effort and courage on my part to break the years of silence despite the shame that I felt. When I had finished, my father laughed out loud and said it was nice to find out that he had such a close relationship with me.

My mother admitted that she had always known about my father's "special relationship" with me, had been jealous of it for many years, and that it was all very depressing for her. I was hurt by my father's reaction and decided to see less of my parents from that point on.

After only a few weeks with the SPK I felt at home and got involved in several working groups. I helped the others make leaflets, which we printed on our small machine. I was feeling good about things in general, and I enjoyed the work there. We had an old record player on which we always played the Ton, Steine, Scherben song "Macht kaputt, was euch kaputt macht" (Destroy What Destroys You), singing along passionately to the lyrics that expressed the way we felt about life. There was always something going on, with groups everywhere having heated discussions about the latest events, the world situation, about books or personal matters. We spent a lot of time organizing protests and demonstrations.

One event that was really important to us was the 1970 victory of Salvador Allende and the Popular Front, in Chile. Was it really possible to carry out a revolution through parliamentary elections? Was it even a revolution? Would the big US corporations stand by and accept their property being seized? What was the Chilean military doing? Lenin was quoted during debates to the effect that "the ruling class will never give up its power without a fight." The Chilean guerrilla organization the MIR supported the Allende government and was carrying out aboveground political work— should they lay down their weapons? Was it a betrayal of the Popular Front to not relinquish their weapons or treachery against the Chilean people and the revolution if they did give them up?

I joined the Marx working group when they were in the middle of the first volume of *Capital*. A few of the eight to ten members in the group had been with the SPK for a long time, while others had joined more recently. I had never read anything by Karl Marx before, and the terms he used in his writings were unfamiliar to me. In the two hours that the working group sessions lasted, those who were more knowledgeable explained the Marxist terminology to the new members and, at the same time, we looked for real examples from everyday life or from what we read in the newspapers, so that we could get an idea of what things like "surplus value," "alienation," "means of production," and "relations of production" actually meant in real terms. The working group offered us a place for discussion where everyone could take part by talking about their own experiences, even people who just happened to chance by. We usually read no more than one-and-a-half pages or so at each session, but, in a few weeks, I learned so much about "dialectics," the method at the heart of Marxist thought, that later in prison I was able to study the weighty tomes of Marx's economic theories on my own without difficulty.

I enjoyed going to the various working groups, because I felt I gained a better understanding of reality there, and because I liked the people, who accepted me as one of them without mistrust. I quickly got over my shyness, felt that I was taken seriously, and got a new lease on life. I learned a great deal in the working groups, a lot of which was quite disturbing. One young woman I had seen a few times in the SPK, who was one of the first patients to belong to the group, tried to commit suicide and was checked into a closed psychiatric unit. I went there with a few friends—it was a large, bleak building situated outside of Heidelberg, with bars on the windows, a prison. We wanted to see her, so we could talk to her and get her out of there. However, the staff wouldn't let us anywhere near her. We were told "only family members." When we demanded to speak to the doctor in charge, we were left to wait for what seemed like an eternity, before a bespectacled man in a white coat came to talk to us.

He was standoffish and abrupt and said we couldn't see her, as talking was pointless, and she needed peace and quiet. We had to return to Heidelberg without having achieved anything.

We were in the middle of the working group dealing with the New Left social analysis of society and reading Arno Plack when we heard screams and a ruckus. We ran out into the hallway, where a young man who had been coming to the SPK for a short time was tearing all of the books off the shelves and smashing the wooden chairs to bits. Other people were trying to calm him down, while he screamed and threatened to beat them up. Nobody dared touch him, and he went back into the secretarial office. There, he turned over a desk and began to pull everything off the shelves. I had spoken to him a few times in the past days, and he had always been very quiet, but he was obviously now having a crisis of some sort. He was big and strong, and everybody was afraid to go near him. Confident that I could approach him and calm him down without having to resort to physical measures, I went into the office. He looked at me in amazement as I began to talk while walking directly toward him, then he hesitated for a moment before he let his arms fall to his sides.

It was during this time that I also developed the need to distance myself from men. It seemed to me that their main interest was sex, while I was looking for something else. This disparity was always there from the very start, and a man, no matter how stupid he was, was always in a position of power. Wherever I went, I came across the same thing— despite what they said, only one thought lingered at the back of men's minds; they wanted to get me into bed as fast as possible. I just wasn't interested in that type of thing anymore. When I was with Gabi I could share my feelings and talk openly about my experiences and what was on my mind. We often felt the same way about things and discovered we had a great deal in common. She was also studying psychology, and we both read Wilhelm Reich, smoked hash, and listened to the same music. We spoke about our pasts, our families, our fears, and our love relationships. She was gentle and headstrong, and, like me, she was trying to find her path in life. We soon developed very tender feelings for one another.

It must have been early February 1971 when Bernd, a friend of mine from university and the Release, came to speak to me. He said he was in touch with some people he trusted who were in trouble with the police and needed passports to escape the manhunt. There was a woman among them who had my build, and he asked if I would give them my passport without reporting it as lost. I didn't hesitate for a second, and I didn't ask any questions. I could tell by the way he asked that it wasn't drug users he was getting my passport for. Although I didn't know Bernd all that well, my intuition, which I had always been able to rely on in the past, told me that he wasn't a snitch or an undercover, and that he could keep his mouth shut. I didn't ask, but I guessed that my passport was for people who had been organizing the armed struggle. I didn't have a clue about what that meant, but I was curious, and it attracted me.

At that time, the state referred to the Red Army Faction (RAF) in derogatory terms as the "Baader-Meinhof Gang" but considered them to be so dangerous that, in late 1971, the Federal Criminal Police Office (Bundeskriminalamt, BKA) set up a "Baader-Meinhof Special Commission" to deal with the group. This taskforce was made up of specialists who had a plan to make the police machinery omnipresent in the years to come. Tens of thousands of people were investigated and countless apartments were searched in 1970–1971 in an attempt to catch the RAF members. There were police checkpoints, street surveillance, and public appeals in the media to identify suspects. Many, mostly young people, were unimpressed by all this. According to one survey carried out in 1971, one in four German citizens of my generation sympathized with the RAF to the degree that they would risk prosecution to hide members from the police. Wanted posters hung in all public buildings and in some shops. When they started appearing in Heidelberg, we snuck around at night to smash the windows of shops that had agreed to put them up.

It was perhaps a week or ten days after this first meeting that Bernd came back again. The people who now had my passport wanted to ask if they could stay in my apartment for a few days, during which time I would have to sleep somewhere else. Once again, I said yes without asking any questions, but I didn't feel as comfortable about it this time. This was going a step further and could be risky for me. If my passport was discovered with the RAF, I could always say that I had lost it or that it had been stolen. However, if I provided my apartment, that would no longer be possible. Nevertheless, my fear was nowhere near as great as my interest in getting to know people who had decided to live a very different kind of life than anything I had known up to that point, and I wanted to learn about their struggle.

On the first night that I was staying somewhere else, I was so anxious I vomited. I was in the process of breaking away from the central tenets and values of my upbringing. It had been hammered into me that crime and violence were inherently "evil," that one did not support people who "broke the law" but handed them over to the police. Although I didn't really know what I was getting myself into, I knew that whatever it was would affect my life considerably, and that things could get dangerous. I had begun to take leave of my previous life.

On that first night, I slept at Bernd's place. He was kind to me and concerned: "I can understand why you need to puke. It's unnerving when you first make contact with the guerrilla. I would love to still have your reaction, instead of having to keep cool and put a calm face on it, as if everything were normal." Although he wasn't supposed to say who had asked to have my apartment, Bernd said it was better that I know.

We spoke about what it would mean for each of us to let the RAF into our lives. Bernd had a career that he enjoyed and that he really didn't want to give up, so going underground was out of the question for him. If anybody discovered that he had been in contact with the RAF, that would mean losing his job. I had begun to doubt what my studies had to offer. What could I do with my degree? Spend my life rummaging about in other people's problems? "Fix" people so that they could be inserted back into working life, which, for me, meant pushing them back into the machinery of exploitation? I felt there must be something else I could do to bring about a more bearable future.

After a few days and nights of living like a vagabond, sometimes at the Release, sometimes at Gabi's place, I told Bernd that I wanted to return to my flat.

Meeting the RAF

When I returned to my flat, I found Ulrike Meinhof, Andreas Baader, Gudrun Ensslin, and Jan-Carl Raspe sitting there. Although I had taken a good look at a wanted poster just days before, I didn't recognize any of them.

Gudrun had an attractive Afro hairstyle that went well with her slim face and big eyes. Ulrike looked small and fragile. She was wearing a headscarf, smoked one cigarette after another, and was constantly fidgeting with her fingers. Andreas had dyed his hair totally blonde, which was very striking, though his black roots were beginning to show. Jan, a tall, thin guy with a very serious but boyish face, was leaning against a wall, while the others sat or lay on my bed. All four of them had very pale faces, as if they never saw sunlight.

"So, what do you want to know?" they asked, grinning at me. I felt uncomfortable, and no particular questions came to mind. "Yeah, well, what you do. I want to get to know you." They wanted to know if I knew who they were, if I recognized them. I shook my head. They asked if they could continue to use my apartment. I nodded yes. So these were the people who had triggered the largest police hunt in the history of the Federal Republic, whose photos were constantly in the press, their names on everybody's lips. I felt intimidated by them, but they also made me feel important.

Andreas, who had been silent up to then, spoke. "To be on the safe side," he said, "it's better anyway if you don't get to know us. And if the pigs ever find out that we were here, the less you know the better." When Andreas talked he came across as assertive, full of energy.

They asked if I knew why they were setting up the urban guerrilla, what their situation was, and if I was aware that being in contact with them could have certain consequences for me, including arrest and prison. I was shy and defiant at the same time but unable to answer any of their questions clearly. There was one thing I did insist on: "If I'm going to let you use my flat, then I want to know what I'm getting into." I wanted to get to know them and find out what they were about, if possible.

They sent me out of the room so they could talk among themselves. After some time, they called me back and said they agreed to my terms. There was one condition, however— that I disappear whenever they had to talk about things that were none of my business. I also wasn't to try to figure out their real identities. Each of them had an assumed name, and that would have to be enough for me. "What is important is what a person does, not what he's called or where he comes from. We all come from the same old shit, which is why we've decided to fight; it's not the individual that counts but the group. In deciding to fight and to live underground, our personal lives have become a function of that fight. What came before doesn't matter anymore."

They told me that in Latin America rural guerrilla groups had formed in the 1960s, and that there was an urban guerrilla movement in Uruguay. In those groups, members of commando units only knew each other by aliases, so that if anyone was arrested they couldn't reveal the names of the others, even under torture.

From then until June 1971, the four of them and Holger Meins came regularly to my small basement apartment on Uferstrasse. They rarely turned up together, mostly coming alone, in twos, or in a group of three to read, write, and talk. They pored over technical drawings and street maps, cleaned their weapons, or just wanted to relax, chill out, and listen to music. They debated, laughed, and joked with one another, for example, about the fact that Ulrike, who had spent most of her previous life at a typewriter, was now the fastest and most skilled at breaking into cars. They all loved Donald Duck comic books and read them together, laughing like children. Andreas and Gudrun often fooled around, giggling like teenagers. If four or five of them were there, and they had time, they cooked together. Once Ulrike made Sauerbraten (marinated beef), one of her favorite meals. She was astonished that I didn't know how to prepare meat in that way, especially as I came from the Rhine region, which was practically the home of Sauerbraten. She seldom drank alcohol, preferring to smoke hash. Her reasoning was that it was better than alcohol, and she could stifle the effect it had on her immediately if need be. Sometimes I bought stuff for her from some people I knew.

I had never met people like them before. Almost everything they did and the way they did it was new to me: their political discussions, the way they handled weapons, their jokes, how they spoke to and treated one another. I had never seen anything like it, not at the Release and not in the SPK or anywhere else before that. They seemed to be connected, to be on the same wavelength, almost as if they shared one mind. I wasn't part of their closeness, of their energy, but the strong bond they had with one another affected me greatly.

While they were busy, I often sat at my desk and filled out index cards for the university's Institute of Psychology. Andreas came over one time, curious about what I was writing. "Why are you doing crap like that?" "It's my job—I have to make a living somehow." "Can't you look for something better?" "Are you going to pay me a salary?" Andreas had to laugh. From that moment on, he accepted it without comment when I sat at the typewriter to type up index cards. He liked having a go at others and provoking them and was pleased when they talked back to him like an equal. When someone gave in to him, he got really annoyed.

They knew, of course, that I was involved with the SPK and had been going there regularly since the beginning of the year. Once, when we were alone, Jan bombarded me with questions about the SPK: what I did there, how I felt there, why I had gone there in the first place, what I thought about it. Then he talked a lot about himself, what he had experienced in the student movement and his work in one of the first Kinderladen in West Berlin, the antiauthoritarian and self-organized childcare spaces that had emerged from the student movement in the late 1960s. It was one of the few longer conversations I had with any of them in those first weeks.

Somewhere along the way, my new friends told me they had come to Heidelberg to make contact with the SPK. This would, of course, have to take place inconspicuously and covertly. Was I willing to help them? "Our first idea was to send Ulrike in disguised with a headscarf and glasses—straight to Wolfgang Huber at the SPK. But the situation's pretty hot—just imagine, there's a massive police search going on for Ulrike, and, right across the street from the pigs' headquarters, she marches straight into the most surveilled building in the whole of Heidelberg. Pretty gutsy. It would be better if you did it. You go in and out of there every day. The only problem is whether or not Huber will believe you when you tell him what you want. What do you think?" My "individual agitations" were with Huber, and I got on well with him. I wanted to at least give it a try.

The SPK's own process of radicalization was well underway in the spring of 1971. Everybody believed that organizing against the state and capital was necessary and legitimate, as was the use of violence. I had no clue, however, that there was already a group within the SPK that had been preparing for armed activities.

At my next appointment with Huber, I broached the subject carefully. I rambled on a bit, beating around the bush, until I finally came to the point: Would the SPK be interested in establishing contact with the RAF? Huber glared at me, gesturing for me to say no more as he pointed to the telephone next to us. He was convinced there was a bug in it. Then he took a piece of paper and wrote: "Write down what you want to ask me while talking about something else at the same time." I was suspicious. Write something down? What was he playing at? That seemed much more dangerous to me than talking. On his piece of paper, he scribbled that we would immediately burn everything we wrote in the ashtray. That made sense to me, and we started writing down our questions and answers on pieces of paper, which we pushed back and forth while Wolfgang talked about illness and its causes in society.

Weeks later, he told me that it was my naive and emotional reaction and my suspicion when he suggested writing things down that had made him believe I actually did have a message for him from the RAF. I never learned the details of what became of this contact. As the public radicalization of the SPK had increased so had the police interest in anybody who regularly visited its premises, so my new friends asked me to tone things down a little; if I was put under surveillance, it would be impossible for them to continue using my flat.

I never knew if or when my six "roommates" would turn up at my place. They didn't have a key, and they didn't want to have one, so it wouldn't be found if one of them got arrested. We had an arrangement that they would only come by in the evenings or at night, as I was almost certain to be home then. They were so careful when entering and leaving the basement on Uferstrasse that my landlord had no idea about the new visitors I was receiving at odd hours. On the other hand, I was no longer able to bring any of my other friends home.

This was most difficult with Gabi. "There are people at my place who wouldn't approve," I said. Gabi had already noticed changes in me, and she knew that I wasn't hiding another love interest from her. She didn't ask, but we both knew that she had some idea about the direction I was moving in. The issue of organizing illegal activities was dealt with pretty openly in Heidelberg in those days, at least in the SPK. She made it clear that that wasn't what she wanted, that it scared her. I respected the way she felt, and it changed nothing in our friendship.

One day Gudrun asked me about Gabi, as she had noticed our special relationship. "Are you intimate with one another, I mean, physically?" When I hesitantly answered yes, Gudrun told me that some of the female RAF comrades had lesbian relationships, and that everybody was okay with it. The student uprisings and the first moves toward autonomous organization among women had also led people to experiment with new lifestyles, with new values and ideas. The women were often ahead of the men in this process of accepting and living out their feelings, and this had given rise to new ways of organizing and understanding their lives. I was amazed at how openly Gudrun talked about everything, and I liked it. It made me feel that my own experiences and feelings were okay.

The newspapers, especially the *Bild* tabloid published by the Springer Corporation, were tripping over themselves to publish articles slandering the women in the RAF; they were all shrews gone mad, authoritarian, crazy about weapons, lesbians, hard, callous, and slaves to Andreas. They even spread the lie that Ulrike had died of a brain tumor. Then they wrote she had committed suicide, because she was depressed about differences within the group. The stories they made up were endless, nasty, unbelievable, and had very little to do with the people in my apartment. I wondered why there was so much hate toward the RAF women and spoke to Gudrun and Ulrike about it. "When women rise up and fight forcefully, it shakes the system to its very foundations. Women are the basis for reproduction in the system. They're supposed to be passive, obedient, accessible, and to make sure that everything stays on an even keel. Women who break out of that mold and refuse to play the role assigned to them, even taking up weapons, are not allowed to exist. That's why they hate us so much."

Ulrike got really upset about the headlines announcing her suicide because of differences within the group. "Those bastards, that's their projection, that's the way things are with them! They're willing to use any of their CIA tricks to undermine us. They follow the same playbook all over the world to discredit revolutionaries and make them look crazy."

I didn't know what my friends did when they were not sitting around my place. I had a vague idea that their goal was to bring about a totally different and fair society and that this could only be achieved using illegal methods. That is why they had weapons, stole cars, robbed banks, and had to avoid being caught by the police and arrested.

All persons residing in Germany have to register at the Residents' Registration Office (Einwohnermeldeamt). Anybody not registered or registered at a false address is in breach of the law and may be prosecuted. As part of its investigation of guerrilla activities, the BKA checked up on apartments, making sure that the people who rented them were properly registered at that address. At that time, RAF members mainly lived in apartments that were rented by people who weren't suspected by the police. While nobody tried to talk me into fighting their fight using their methods, they did ask if I was willing to rent an apartment for them in another city. I agreed to do it.

Gudrun and Andreas stayed at my flat to look after my dog. They weren't very pleased about it, but what was I supposed to do with him? I went by train to Hamburg, where Holger picked me up at the station and brought me to a small hotel. We bought a pile of newspapers and started checking out the classifieds. He told me that apartments in high-rise complexes best suited their needs, as the people who lived there didn't know and didn't care what went on next door, making it easy to come and go without arousing suspicion. We soon found a suitable place on Mexikoring in the City Nord district, a rapidly growing area on the outskirts where office buildings and several residential blocks had sprung up. "That's exactly what we're looking for," Holger grinned, "Andreas and Ulrike could stand in the lift next to a wanted poster without their make-up on, and nobody would recognize them. The people who live there are too busy thinking about their work stress or the problems with their old lady and the kids." I liked his dry sense of humor and his way of getting to the point with short and snappy sentences. "Okay, call the number and tell them you want to look at the place."

The next day—it was early March 1971—I went to the offices of the housing association. I was wearing a skirt and had put on some make-up and tied my hair back in a neat ponytail. "You should come across as uninteresting, boring, like a secretary," Holger said, giving me some money. One of the people from the housing association accompanied me to the apartment; I told him I was starting work in Hamburg in April, which was why I had to leave Heidelberg. While we were on our way there, I kept a constant lookout to see if the police were following us or if anything untoward happened, something Holger had been emphatic about. It seemed absurd to watch out for possible police surveillance. I wouldn't recognize them unless they were two feet behind me in a marked car. The place was a small one-room apartment. I signed the rental contract and assured the man I would pay the rent every month punctually by postal money order, and then went with my ID card to the residents' registration office and put down Hamburg as my second place of residence. I would only ever be in that Mexikoring apartment on one other occasion, four months later, after I had burned my ID documents and personal papers to go "underground."

After the Hamburg expedition, Holger came to my place in Heidelberg a few times and stayed the night. We felt good together. The first time I met him in my flat, I could see in his eyes that he liked me. My first thought was: "So, just like all the other guys, only interested in outward appearances." But then I realized that he thought about me in a way that nobody else in the group did, that he was trying to understand who I was and what it was I needed. He was a very visual person, and he also had the unusual talent of being completely in the moment. I felt a kind of freedom when we were together that I had never known before. When I was with him, I felt good, but when he wasn't there, I didn't miss him. He knew I had other love interests but showed no sign of jealousy or possessiveness. I liked that. I hated jealousy, and I couldn't stand it when somebody acted like I belonged to them.

What attracted me to the RAF comrades most was their uncompromising seriousness. They lived the way they talked and didn't play games. There was no difference between words and action in their world. I still couldn't fully understand the political dimension of what they believed in, but I was fascinated by their commitment to their cause. This was something Gudrun later referred to as "deeply felt free will." I looked on, intrigued by the way they argued with one another with an openness and directness I had never experienced before and how they fought for themselves and for everyone in the group.

One afternoon, Andreas, Gudrun, and Jan came to my place. I was reading and listening to music when they arrived. All three were on edge. They had been doing target practice in the woods, and in exercises like that each of them was assigned a specific task: Andreas was responsible for the stolen car and the machine gun that was always within reach during car trips. Jan was in charge of keeping a lookout and securing the "shooting range," and Gudrun was supposed to make sure that nothing was left behind when they were finished. But when they got to the flat and emptied their bags, Gudrun saw that Andreas's pistol was missing. They had left it behind in the forest, and Andreas was furious. Now they would have to go out again to retrieve the weapon, which might have already been found by somebody. Andreas blamed Gudrun, saying she was good for nothing. "You're a complete idiot. What do you have a brain for? If we hit a roadblock now, I'll have to let them shoot me." Gudrun remained absolutely calm. Andreas continued screaming, and I was afraid he was going to hit Gudrun. Gudrun said nothing but cringed in the face of this barrage of insults and threatening behavior.

I was shocked by this scene and angry at Andreas for his screaming and threats. I was immediately on Gudrun's side: "Leave her alone!" I shouted at Andreas. Later, Gudrun took me aside. "Andreas screwed up too, he's responsible for his own gun. And then all that screaming—what a waste of energy. But, you know, the worst thing of all for me is that I put up with it. I should have argued back at least. It was crap of me just to give in to him and not react. You know what I mean?" I didn't really understand.

When Andreas discovered somebody had made a mistake, he could be very aggressive and insulting. He lived according to the standards he set for others, which is why everyone in the group accepted his sharp tongue and his angry outbursts. At that time, I still didn't know how hard it would be for me to deal with his criticisms.

One night, Andreas and another member of the group came to my place. They had been out stealing cars. While they were in the middle of trying to break into one, a policeman suddenly arrived on the scene, gun drawn. Andreas, who had stayed back in the lookout car, climbed out silently, snuck up behind the policeman with his pistol drawn, then threatened him, while shouting to the other guy, "Quick, get out of here!" Both of them ran to the car, Andreas taking the first steps backwards with his pistol still aimed at the policeman. Then they jumped into the car and sped off. No shots were fired.

Now both of them were sitting panting breathlessly in my apartment. They kept on going over to the window, nervously checking the street outside. Andreas was furious and accused the other guy of freezing. "Why didn't you draw your weapon? Or throw yourself behind the car? Or both?" He turned toward me: "He just stood there like some stupid animal waiting for a harness." Then back to the guy: "What's wrong with you? Do you want to fight or not? That pig could have easily got you. How are we supposed to rely on a guy like you who cowers like a scared dog when it matters most? Get it together." Andreas sat down and then jumped up again in a fit of rage. The other guy just lit up one Gauloise after another and didn't say a thing. He must have felt like shit.

The use of weapons was discussed again and again. When was it okay to shoot and at whom? This was a question that first came up for intense discussion when a man was seriously injured during the operation that freed Andreas from prison in May 1970. Ulrike in particular spoke about the limits to her own use of violence, returning to the question over and over again in public declarations. In the first RAF manifesto, *The Urban Guerrilla Concept*, which had mainly been written by Ulrike, she gave an emphatic no in response to the question that was often asked: Would the action to free Andreas have gone ahead in the same way if those freeing him had foreseen the injury or death of bystanders?

However, this paper did not appear until eleven months after Andreas had been freed, meaning that many on the left had already made up their minds about the RAF—people like my boyfriend and Armin Golzem. They were far more likely to be aware of the statement Ulrike had made on tape three weeks after Andreas had been freed, in which she said: "[W]e say the cops are swine, we say a man in uniform is a pig, not a human being, so we must neutralize him. I mean, we are in conflict with him and we have nothing to say to him ... of course there may be shooting."

One day, Ulrike came alone. She had her typewriter and a great pile of papers with her. She sat down and began to write, working day and night, hardly sleeping. She chain-smoked and drank coffee by the liter. The relentless pace at which she typed out page after page impressed me. I would never have been able to work like that, and I didn't know anyone who had the same drive and focus she did when she was working on something. She gave me a few pages to read: "I want to hear what you think." The title was *The Urban Guerrilla Concept*. I plodded my way through the text. It took a lot of effort on my part to understand what she was saying. When I was finished, I handed the pages back to her. "I think it's very good," I said. Ulrike was annoyed. "I don't want to hear compliments, shit, I want to know your opinion." I was unable to deliver.

Ulrike and Andreas discussed the text for hours on end, arguing with one another but also laughing together. They enjoyed going up against each other, and their discussions could be very fierce. If Ulrike felt that Andreas was being too harsh, she would snap at him, "Then you write it!" And he would laugh, telling her, "You know quite well that I can't put things the way you can. I have a good idea of what has to be said, but nobody can write it like you."

When the friends debated, things often got pretty intense, it was like a wrestling match. It was how they forced each other to think more sharply and to express their thoughts more precisely. Andreas in particular was restless, always searching for something. He couldn't stay in the same spot from one second to the next. His head was full of ideas.

I asked Ulrike about the paragraph about freeing Andreas. "Yes," Ulrike said, "we have to answer the question that people are always asking us. It was a mistake to hand over the tape recording with the phrase 'of course there may be shooting' on it without having discussed it again beforehand," she added.

In *The Urban Guerrilla Concept* there were paragraphs that I especially liked, for example:

> [The student movement's] identity was not based on class struggle here, but rather on the knowledge that they were part of an international movement, that they were dealing with the same class enemy as the Viet Cong, the same paper tigers, the same pigs.

And:

> We don't count on terror and fascism provoking a spontaneous antifascist mobilization, nor do we think that legality is always corrupt. We understand that our work offers pretexts [for intolerance and oppression]. … Regarding other pretexts that result from the fact that we are communists, whether communists organize and struggle will depend on whether terror and repression produce only fear and resignation, or whether they produce resistance, class hatred, and solidarity, and whether or not everything goes smoothly for imperialism. It depends on whether communists are so stupid as to tolerate everything that is done to them, or whether they will use legality, as well as other methods, to organize illegality, instead of fetishizing one over the other.

The text referred in several places to the Black Panthers in the United States and, because they were mentioned so often during discussions, especially by Gudrun, I asked her about them one time when we were alone. Gudrun told me there was a solidarity network in West Germany for GIs that she had worked with in the 1960s. She had organized apartments, papers, money, and clandestine border crossings for GIs who had deserted because they didn't want to fight in Vietnam. She met Black soldiers who were Black Panthers, and who were trying to organize resistance within the US Army. During discussions with these Black Panthers, who put out an underground newspaper, she found out more about the history and the ideas of various Black organizations in the US. The suppression of the Black Panthers had given rise to a Black guerrilla, the Black Liberation Army. There was also another guerrilla organization, the Weathermen, which, like the RAF, had developed out of the student movement and the protests against the Vietnam War. Gudrun said she would love to fly to the US and meet up with the Weathermen. "We think their development is very similar to ours. The Weathermen and we from the RAF have come to very similar conclusions and practices, because certain conditions are the same. West Germany and the US are today the most highly developed industrial countries with a strong labor aristocracy and corrupt trade union leadership. There, like here, neofascism, consumer terror, and media control are widespread."

It was from Gudrun that I learned that in Europe the most intense discussions were taking place among the Italian comrades, many of whom had left the traditionally strong Communist Party and some of whom had begun to organize an armed political movement. Their ideas were aimed primarily at the already existing broad Italian workers' movement. Those who saw themselves operating more in an internationalist context, as the RAF did, rejected urban guerrillas carrying out armed activities at the present time. That had been a hard blow for them. Gudrun, Ulrike, and Andreas often spoke of their trips to Italy, where they had

had so many discussions. I can't remember the details of what these discussions were about, because, at the time, I had difficulty following the gist of what they were talking about.

There was one other passage that I liked in the RAF paper, where they quoted from Lenin. "The fact is that the working masses are roused to a high pitch of excitement by the social evils in Russian life, but we are unable to gather, if one may so put it, and concentrate all these drops and streamlets of popular resentment" is compared to the situation at the time in West Germany: "The drops and streamlets based on the horrors [here] have long been collected by the Springer Corporation, to which they then add new horrors."

On the afternoon of April 30, 1971, Jan and Holger came in with a big bundle of copies of *The Urban Guerrilla Concept*. The RAF's symbol, the three letters above a machine gun, stood out clearly, and the text had been printed on good quality paper. I liked it a lot. They were both glowing with pride and joy. Jan told me that the newspaper was to be distributed at the May Day demo the next day. "Do you think you could leave a bundle of them at the college without anybody seeing you? You have to avoid getting your fingerprints on them, no matter what. The best thing would be to take them wrapped in newspaper and then, when you've laid them down, pull the newspaper away carefully. Other people will be distributing them in different places at the same time. Everything has to happen simultaneously so that nobody gets caught. You have to lay them down at exactly the right moment—not a minute too soon or too late." I was as proud of the newspaper as if I had contributed to its writing myself. The top one was my copy and, in the evening, I sat down and read it once again in peace and quiet. Of course I wanted to help distribute it. The next morning, I was excited as I left the house with my bundle wrapped up in a plastic bag. When I got to the college, I was far too early. I wandered around for a while, my heart racing and my hands beginning to shake. Finally, the time came to lay down the bundle. I hesitated: Should I hang around nearby to see what happened? My nervousness won the day. I felt as if everybody could see I was leaving a bundle of forbidden newspapers there. I walked around a little and then returned to my apartment.

I continued to go to the SPK, to the work groups, taking part in discussions and offering my support against the imminent ban of the group. I took part in the night watches, which were designed to fend off a surprise eviction by the police. For nights on end, we discussed the imperialist system and its devastating consequences. I learned that US troops were involved in a brutal war, and not just in Vietnam, because they believed they had the right to decide what other people should think and how they should live their lives. The history of US interventions throughout the world was a long one, and something I had known very little about prior to that. Why did I know so little about it? Why had there been so little resistance against it? To justify thirty thousand US soldiers marching into the Dominican Republic, US President Johnson had declared: "We cannot and will not permit the establishment of another Communist government in the Western Hemisphere!" They always dragged out the word democracy, but when it came to their economic and political interests, they showed up with bombs, tanks, and torturers. I found hate and anger welling up inside me as I realized I had been lied to all my life. I was now beginning to understand the causes and the contexts of historical events, and I wanted to do something about it.

Tapping into suffering to find strength to fight back was something I could identify with. I could relate to people picking up their loneliness and desperation like a stone and hurling it against the root causes—causes that lay within capitalist society. We considered illness to be a central source of revolutionary ideas, "Turn illness into a weapon!"

being the slogan of the SPK. At one demonstration in the center of Heidelberg against the Vietnam War and the invasion of Cambodia by US troops, one after the other the speakers were talking about the situation in Vietnam, the Viet Cong's struggle, and the crimes of the US troops, when suddenly I grabbed the microphone. "And what's with our struggle here at home?" I shouted, "Why are you always talking about other places and not about the revolution here in Europe?" The language we used in our pamphlets was becoming increasingly radical. The revolution had to come today, and anybody who didn't understand this was an idiot or an exploiter. We looked down on other leftists who didn't see things the way we did.

Through the SPK and the RAF, in a short space of time, I had come to know a very different kind of life. There was lots I couldn't talk about, as doing so would put certain people at risk. Andreas, Gudrun, Ulrike, and Holger warned me when they thought I wasn't being careful enough. They were the most wanted "criminals" in West Germany, and they had been using my place for weeks. Nobody was allowed to visit me at home anymore, because I never knew if or when they would turn up. I was supposed to be suspicious of every new person I met and, if possible, tell nobody what my name was or where I lived. I tried to avoid my landlord, whose window I had to pass by to get into my flat. I found these precautions difficult to follow, feeling that they restricted my freedom, but I understood why they were necessary and kept to the rules.

Various people who knew me, not just Gabi, noticed what was going on. One friend from university who I really liked surprised me one day with a marriage proposal. "Let's get married, finish off our studies together, and then have children." That was exactly what I didn't want, and when he had expressed his three wishes, that became clearer to me than ever before. I was already starting on my new path in life. I didn't know where it would take me. It might end in prison or death, but for the first time in my life I felt I was living the way I wanted to.

However, I wasn't given very much time to think this through. All of a sudden, things heated up and events took on a momentum of their own.

At the end of June 1971, there was a shootout with the police in some woods outside of Heidelberg, and several members of the SPK were arrested. We organized our last meeting, appealing to people to take up the armed struggle. We regarded the arrest of eight or so SPK members as an arbitrary act of retaliation by the police, and to demonstrate how we felt about it some of us tore the photos out of our ID cards and replaced them with photos of Che or Ho Chi Minh. "Mahler, Meinhof, Baader—they are our cadre!" we shouted, as we called for clandestine structures to be established. We read out loud from the RAF's *The Urban Guerrilla Concept*: "The class analysis we require cannot be developed without revolutionary practice or revolutionary initiative." We shouted these slogans in the university lecture theatre, without having any real idea about what we were saying. The process of radicalization in the SPK had happened extremely fast. Our willingness to act, our conviction that the political could not be separated from the personal, found their direct expression in the slogans: "Destroy what destroys you" and, expressing our desire to turn all kinds of illness into weapons against society, "Throw your kidney stones at the banks!"

July saw the second wave of arrests, and the SPK was forced to disband. A police surveillance car suddenly appeared outside my place, but my friends from the RAF had already taken their leave from me days before the shootout.

I considered my options. Completing my studies didn't seem to make any sense. The SPK had broken up, and the people I liked had either gone underground or had been arrested. The same could happen to me if the police discovered I had rented an apartment in Hamburg for the RAF. If they checked my papers, they would find out I had entered a second place of residence on my ID card. I didn't want to just hang around at home and wait to be arrested. I had to say goodbye to my past, my parents, my friends, and my life as it was. All I had now was the RAF.

I went to Bernd and told him I wanted to burn all bridges to my previous life, and that I intended to join the RAF. While he respected my decision, he still tried dissuade me. "Aren't you afraid? There are other ways to get things done. If the cops find out about the place in Hamburg, you'll get a few months in jail. That might be crap, no doubt about it, but don't you realize what'll happen if you go the other way? The shootouts, arrests, going down for a long time. Is that what you want?"

Afraid? Unlike him, I had no fear. Instead, I felt strong in a way I had never felt before.

I spoke with Gabi, and we agreed she would move everything out of my place gradually and discreetly. At some point, she would tell my landlord that I had had a bad accident and wasn't coming back. Gabi and I burned all my photos, personal belongings, and letters in the toilet. I knew where my life was now taking me: to Hamburg and the flat on Mexikoring.

Going Underground

That very same day, Holger showed up at the place on Mexikoring. The RAF hadn't been using it for some time now, as the comrades were worried that I might be arrested, and then the police would be checking it out. Because of this, they were in the process of vacating the place.

Holger brought me to another apartment, and after a while Andreas and Gudrun came to talk to me. The curtains, long swathes of dark cloth, were drawn across the windows, and we were sitting in semi-darkness. Neither of them seemed very pleased to see me, and Andreas came straight to the point: "So tell us what it is you want. What were you thinking of, just turning up here like that?" I told them that the police had been watching my flat, and it seemed I might be arrested at any time. I thought that would seem like an acceptable reason to him, but he wanted to hear more. "What is it you think you can do here with us? Is there anything you can do that seems like a good idea to you?" I didn't have a clue. "Then tell us what you think about us politically. What is your analysis of the situation? Go on, tell us!" As I stood there, tongue-tied, not even able to get out two words on the subject, Andreas grew increasingly annoyed.

He was pacing back and forth, smoking Gauloises and ranting. "How could you be so stupid? Did you think you could just turn up here and become one of us? Who do you think we are? Do you think this is a game? Don't tell me you can't come up with anything better than that!" The truth of it was I hadn't really given much thought to the matter, and when this eventually became clear, he was even more irritated. "If there wasn't something real they could arrest you for, we would send you back to Heidelberg today. What are we supposed to do with you now? For fuck's sake, this is going to cause nothing but problems."

Although I didn't realize it at the time, he was right.

I stayed at that place for a few days, until Holger came and picked me up. We drove to Frankfurt and stayed in a safehouse with a woman who worked with the RAF. At night, Holger and I went out, and he showed me how to find cars to steal. They had to be parked in dark places, and the parking space had to be some distance from any apartment blocks from where residents might observe the theft, as well as far away from any police station, as, otherwise, the police could be on the scene quickly if alerted. You also had to be familiar with the schedule of the police's nightly rounds in the area.

Holger showed me the tools he used to break into cars: there was a kind of corkscrew with two screw threads that were welded together in opposite directions to one another. After breaking into the car, you inserted this into the ignition, twisting it out completely and quickly, but without using too much force.

We spoke about the fact that Holger had a weapon, while I was unarmed. He thought it was a bad idea to be out together under these conditions, however, for the time being, I wasn't supposed to have a gun. Holger told me that if the police turned up, I had to throw myself to the ground immediately and not move an inch. I would then be arrested, but wouldn't get more than a few months in prison. To be honest, I wasn't that eager to carry a weapon.

After a few days, we returned to Hamburg. When we got there, I learned from Ulrike that three other people from the SPK had left Heidelberg and turned up wanting to join the underground. She suggested that those three and I form our own unit. The other SPK members didn't have any more of an idea about what to do or any more experience than I did.

However, the RAF thought it would be better if we developed our own thing with their help.

I knew the three from the SPK but hadn't had much to do with them up to then. The RAF allocated the four of us a place to live. It was cramped, and we sat around not really knowing what to do with one another. None of us had a clear idea about what should come next. We were "legal illegals," still running around with our own ID cards. The comrades from the RAF really hoped we could pull something together. Despite the fact that we all came from the SPK, we hardly knew each other, and, thrown together in this situation, nothing really clicked for us. The other two women and I found the one guy to be a bit of an idiot, but that didn't bring us any closer together.

Ulrike came to see us with Carmen Roll. Ulrike gave us some money and said, "That's revolutionary money, and I want to know exactly what you spend it on, it's not to be squandered." She was strict, assertive, and impatient, but Carmen, who we knew from the SPK, was easier to get along with. She was a round bundle of energy, fresh and witty. Both women advised us to systematically travel and walk around Hamburg with a city map, to get to know the city we were living in. Ulrike said we should start breaking into cars and told us what places and parts of town were best.

After that, we often went out in pairs, walking and walking until our feet hurt, looking for fast cars. Ulrike brought us the "corkscrew" and, using an old ignition lock, she showed us how it worked and how we could jumpstart cars. We should search for a "double" of the car we wanted to steal: a car of the same make, color, design, and year. Once we had found it, we had to get a hold of the car owner's details, for example, by calling the motor vehicle registration office saying we were from the automobile inspections department and that we wanted all of the information they had on the car owner. This information was needed for the vehicle documents. We now needed a quiet place, a garage would be best, to keep the car in right after we stole it. Ulrike checked out the place we had chosen to make sure we hadn't made any mistakes. There had to be a getaway car in case anything went wrong; the RAF gave us one "on loan." We could listen to the police scanner in it, so that we would know if we had been discovered by someone and reported. We got a hold of thin gloves that we could wear and still work well without leaving fingerprints.

When the time finally came and we left the flat in a group of three, I was really nervous. Two of us crept up to the car we had picked out—the only one we stole at that time—while I parked our getaway car nearby where the others could see me. It seemed like an eternity before they opened the small side window with the thin piece of wire. All of a sudden, another car drove by and the two of them had to throw themselves behind "our" car. After they finally got inside, everything went very fast. They drove to the agreed place, a quiet dead-end street in another part of town, with me right behind. We unscrewed the license plates and put on new ones we had stolen from another car some time before. The next day we bought a new ignition lock and, after making sure that the stolen car wasn't under observation, installed it. Then we moved the car every day to avoid detection.

Even after this first joint activity, things didn't really pick up among the four of us. There were no conversations, there was nothing we wanted to do together, and we had no ideas about what political action we could carry out as a group.

We sat down one day with Jan-Carl to talk about getting some money. "It has to be clear that we won't keep giving you money forever. You have to get on your own feet. Have you thought about it? There are various possibilities: a money courier, a cash messenger from a supermarket, or a bank. You have to think about what you can manage and see if it's doable."

He suggested looking around in the Greater Hamburg area, maybe Hildesheim. The RAF had already begun to look for options there and could give us a few tips. "No matter what you decide, always work using the city map. Where is the nearest cop shop, and how long do they need to get to where you are if somebody warns them. The most important thing is your escape route, where can you park the getaway car, how can you hide from view immediately, if necessary, where can you change cars without being noticed, and where can you stash the money." These were the basic rules for fundraising activities.

We alternated travelling to Hildesheim in groups of two, leaving by train early in the morning. We had been instructed that, if possible, we should leave right after getting up and throw the tickets away immediately, so that if we got arrested nobody would know where we'd come from. We got on the train at Hamburg-Harburg, travelled to somewhere near Hanover or out to the suburbs and, from there, continued in the direction of Hildesheim. It was getting toward the end of summer, and temperatures were very warm when we arrived in Hildesheim around midday. Our first target was the main checkout at a department store, and we tried to find out what the pattern of transporting their receipts was. Jan had said that the money from the main checkout was often brought to the bank at midday, and the messenger who brought it always used one particular staircase, which led from the personnel department to the street. One of us took up position as discreetly as possible on the other side of the street, opposite the entrance, from where the staircase could be viewed, and waited there for half an hour. To avoid arousing suspicion, we weren't to hang around any longer than that.

We did this for several days but learned nothing. The whole undertaking was very complicated and too difficult to continue. The journey from Hamburg took a long time, and we didn't know anyone in Hildesheim who could give us information or help us in any other way. After a while, watching the department store from the street became too obvious and, therefore, too risky, so we began checking out banks. I often left Hamburg in the morning, returning in the evenings feeling tired and frustrated. Finally, we found a bank that seemed suitable for a robbery: the cash desk only had a very low glass barrier that would be easy to jump over, there was obviously a lot of money behind the counter, the police station was quite a distance away, and there were various possible getaway routes. We told the RAF about our observations, and one of them travelled to Hildesheim to make sure we hadn't overlooked anything. The next step was to rent an apartment. I often went to Hildesheim alone or with one of the women from our small "group" to check out apartment-finding organizations or to look through the local newspapers for accommodations being advertised.

Travelling by train so much was a pain. I often felt tired and chewed endlessly on gummy bears, ruining my teeth in the process. I just couldn't see any point to what we were doing. My head was empty. I had no imagination. Everything was gray.

In between, we travelled to our home towns to stay in touch with friends and see if we could find support for clandestine organizing. I visited my parents in Bonn, so that they wouldn't go looking for me in Heidelberg. I also saw a few old friends, but I had already known beforehand that none of them would choose the same path as me. I asked them what they were doing, only half-listening to their answers. I said almost nothing about what I was doing and generally left as soon as I could.

In Prison

October 23, 1971. I woke up after my first night in prison to an unpleasant, cold, bluish light. It was coming from a small lamp behind some wire mesh in an alcove in the wall. It would stay on every night. Before I had gone to sleep, they had taken the blue prison uniform from me and given me a white nightshirt that barely fit me.

When I was brought out for my first walk around the yard, they cuffed my hands behind my back. They said I had to be put in handcuffs every time I left my cell, because I was violent and extremely dangerous. Whenever they opened the cell door, they were always accompanied by a male guard. Later, they had two female guards stand in front of the door at all times. For half an hour every day, they brought me out into a tiny triangular yard between the outer wall and the women's block to get some fresh air. It was impossible to walk properly, because no matter which way I went, I was standing right in front of a wall. Armed guards surrounded the yard and observed every step I took. I hated them more than any other guards, and their hatred for me was just as apparent.

I had been locked up in a cell at the end of a long corridor right next to the administrative wing. The cells next to mine and those above and below me were empty. None of the other prisoners were allowed to speak or communicate with me in any way. Before my cell door could be opened, all the other prisoners had to leave the corridor.

There was an opening about the size of a book in my door, covered with a tightly meshed grill. I was observed through this opening twenty-four hours a day at irregular intervals:

when I was awake, when I was asleep, when I was reading, writing, or thinking about things, when I was exercising or sitting on the toilet, when I was sad, angry, or wanted to cry.

I was under tremendous pressure, surrounded by walls and weapons, always under observation and subject to their control. I expected to be ambushed at any time, and the stress made me lose my voice, leaving only a whisper. Before entering prison, I had often gotten in my own way, feeling insecure and indecisive. But now I discovered a great strength within that I hadn't known was there. I had to defend myself, and I knew I could do it.

I didn't know anything about life in prison or about the experiences of other prisoners. In those first days, I thought that every prisoner was treated the way I was. At that time, nobody knew much about isolation practices. Up until my arrest, there had only been a few arrests of members of the guerrilla or other left-wing revolutionary groups. It wasn't until I talked to the lawyers the comrades had arranged to represent me that I found out how unusual the conditions of my imprisonment were. The judge overseeing my case had ordered "strict solitary confinement; Margrit Schiller's hands must be handcuffed behind her back whenever she is outside of her cell; she must also remain handcuffed during the exercise period; the cell must be illuminated day and night, without a break; all fixtures must be removed from the cell; prison clothes instead of private clothing; the prison clothes must be removed at night." These kinds of strict conditions had always existed for prisoners who rebelled; however, their application in such a systematic way from the very first day and on a long-term basis was special treatment used specifically to target members of the guerrilla.

My lawyers did everything they could within the limits of the law but were rebuffed by every level of the judiciary, right up to the Federal Court of Justice (Bundesgerichtsghof, BGH)—the highest court in Germany, similar to the Supreme

Court in the United States. They filed a complaint against the judge who had ordered solitary confinement on the grounds that "[t]here is no justification whatsoever for this measure. The only explanation for this is that the person Margrit Schiller is to be systematically and deliberately tortured, deprived of her freedom and degraded, her punishment a public example designed to deter others and with the aim of wearing down the prisoner before she testifies." Furthermore, they added, the circumstances surrounding my confinement were "an appalling follow-up to the so-called press conference at which the Hamburg chief superintendent arranged for the arrestee Margrit Schiller to be brought in violently, like an animal. The direction that has been pursued here must be recognized clearly for what it is. It is unacceptable that judges and officers of the law, who were sworn in on the basis of the constitutional state and the constitution, are today guilty of perpetrating acts of brutality and violence that blatantly disregard all of the precepts of our Basic Law, and which, up until now, were only conceivable as activities of the former Gestapo and openly fascist regimes."

From the moment of my arrest, I was treated as an enemy of the state, despite the fact that the Federal Public Prosecutor General correctly acknowledged that I was only "on the margins of the Baader-Meinhof Group." Despite that, the SPD Hamburg judiciary was to spare no expense. After my arrest, the regular constant security patrols at the prison were reinforced by ten men and twenty guard dogs, and the outer walls of Holstenglacis prison were so brightly lit by floodlights that nighttime was as bright as day. The legal authorities justified these measures by saying they had to prevent my being freed by the guerrilla.

The directives issued by the custodial judge also meant that after visits from my lawyers I had to strip naked in the presence of two female guards and be subjected to a body search. During these, I tensed up all over. Making me

undress was meant to rob me of my dignity and force me
into submission. I concentrated on making a suit of armor
out of my face and skin, a suit of armor to deflect their gaze.
I remained cold and rigid on the outside, while on the inside,
I was summoning every ounce of strength to defend myself.
It was also new for the female guards in Hamburg to have to
strip-search a prisoner on a daily basis. Some of them were
embarrassed and tried to avoid looking at me. I had to put
up with this indignity for several weeks, until the District
Court overruled the practice.

A few days after my arrest, I received my first mail. Many
of the letters came from people I didn't know at all. The
choking incident in front of the cameras the day after my
arrest had set off a fierce public debate about what limits
there should be on the police and about violations of human
dignity and the constitutional rule of law. Many letters
expressed outrage and solidarity. Individuals, lawyers, and
groups lodged complaints. The undersecretary of state in
the North-Rhine Westphalia Ministry of Justice at the time,
Ulrich Klug, called the whole thing a "brutal act of police
violence," a stand that was widely applauded. One man who
worked at the Hamburg docks accused the chief superintendent of using "Gestapo methods"; he was fined for libel several months later as a result. I also received letters in which
people expressed their respect for those who had begun to
engage in armed struggle.

I had become a public figure overnight. The popular
weekly *Stern* magazine printed a story over several pages
with photos my parents gave them.

Curious and friendly, the other female prisoners watched
me from their cell windows whenever I was in the yard on
my own. And when they had their yard time I would watch
them from my cell, laughing and chatting together. Despite
the fact that it was forbidden to have contact with me, more
than one of them called out a greeting or flashed me the

victory sign. In the evenings, when everybody was locked in their cells, the women talked with one another from window to window. They also called out to me, asking how I was doing, where I came from, and if I would be freed soon.

I didn't have my own radio, but there was a speaker in every cell, so we could hear whatever radio program the prison director had chosen. When they played good music, I plugged in my earphones, turned the volume up full, and danced as freely as the cord would allow. Music touched me at the core of my being; it gave me energy and pushed away the walls a little. Every song reminded me of people, moments, feelings. Rod Stewart's voice, for example, reminded me that Ulrike always turned up the radio whenever one of his songs came on. Later, she would be annoyed with herself for having liked his music so much.

Life in a prison cell felt somehow familiar to me. What I had experienced more than anything during my childhood and when I was a teenager was being alone. That had only changed in the past few years at the university and in Heidelberg. In prison, strangely enough, at first, I felt less alone than I had at home. However, this would prove deceptive; I didn't know anything about complete isolation yet, about the prison within the prison.

I had refused to make any statement whatsoever on the night I was arrested. The detention order showed that the court hoped to wear me down through harsh treatment.

After a few days in my cell, my daily routine was interrupted. I had already had my time in the yard, when a guard came to get me, leading me into the empty cell next to mine. Two officers from the BKA were sitting there: "We would like to talk to you in peace and quiet, one human being to another. You know that you are facing charges of murder and attempted murder, as well as charges in connection with the shootout in Freiburg, but things don't have to stay that way. Maybe you can help us understand exactly what happened.

We don't want an intelligent young woman like you to have to live in these conditions any longer. Please, sit down! Tell us who you were with at the Bremgarten highway carpark." I listened to them, standing all the while. Then, quietly, I told them that I didn't have anything to say, not a single thing. I turned and walked past the guard who was waiting at the door and back into my cell.

About a week later, on my way back to my cell from the yard, the men from the BKA tried again. They addressed me in front of the entire team of guards who had been summoned for the occasion. I was furious and screamed that they should leave me in peace, and that I would throw the first object I could lay hands on at their heads if they came back.

They left me in peace after that, but the judiciary tried to find other ways to get at me. One morning, in early December 1971, I had just exchanged my night shirt for prison overalls, when I was abruptly told, "Pack only what you really need. You're being transferred. We'll send your other things later." I asked where I was going but received no answer. Transferred? Why? My lawyers hadn't said a word about this. As usual, I was handcuffed and several guards led me to an unmarked car that was accompanied by a convoy of vehicles, with a marked car at each end. They raced through the city, blue lights flashing and sirens blaring, running all the red lights, and drove to a sports field where a helicopter was waiting with its rotor blades already spinning. I was surrounded by an enormous police presence, all of them with their weapons pointed at me. I didn't know whether to laugh or cry. The police, all of them plainclothes, were nervous and on edge, scared there would be an attempt to free me. The massive police presence when prisoners from the guerrilla were transferred was meant to show that any attempt to free prisoners would be met with a violent response. But it also represented a vast display of power.

The helicopter flew some way toward the highway and landed on a strip of grass in the middle of an intersection. Several unmarked police vehicles were waiting there, and this convoy then drove for hours to the south. The individual vehicles maintained radio contact with one another, and there were checkpoints along the way. I tried to absorb everything I could see of the countryside whizzing past, the cars and the people, suspecting that I wouldn't be seeing any countryside and only very few people for quite a long time.

The places we stopped at, for example, to go for a pee, had been carefully selected beforehand. Everywhere we went, marked cars were waiting for us. When the policemen got out, they took their machine guns, which otherwise lay on the floor as we drove.

After one of these pit stops, we suddenly heard a loud bang. The two policemen to the right and left of me and the one in the passenger seat up front grabbed their machine guns, ducked, and pushed me down between the seats. The driver swerved and pulled over to the side of the road, tires screeching. Two of the policemen jumped out of the car with their guns ready to shoot, throwing themselves into the ditches at the side of the road. The next car in the convoy braked and the policemen in it jumped out with their machine guns similarly ready to shoot. Then one of them exclaimed, "The tire! Look at the tire!" It took a moment or two before everybody realized what had happened and began to laugh, relieved. One of the car's back tires had blown out, sounding like a shot. I had to remain sitting in the car while they changed the tire, then the journey continued.

Late in the afternoon, we reached a large, old building: Aichach near Augsburg. It was the ruins of a bleak old monastery that had been converted into a prison. A fitting change, I thought bitterly. I had to hand over my own clothes, which had been given to me for the journey, and was given a dark blue prison dress with a white collar and a white apron in return. It was far too small, and I refused to wear it. All the other prisoners had been locked away at the time of my arrival. The female guards I passed on my way to my new cell either looked away as if I had the evil eye or stared at me as if I was an actual monster who they would rather not bump into outside those walls.

The following morning, a fat, disgusting man, the prison director, came into my cell. He said he didn't know why they had brought me there. He also didn't know how long I was to stay. However, as long as I was there, he said, I had to strictly follow his instructions, and "I hope you are away from here soon." With that, he disappeared.

The cell was a dark hole. Everything was bolted to the walls and nothing could be moved. I was freezing, as the only heat came from a pipe that exited the ceiling, went straight down the wall, and then disappeared into the floor. Hot water flowed through the pipe mornings and evenings, but it stayed cold the rest of the time, as most of the prisoners worked outside of their cells during the day.

That first morning, they brought me to another cell where two plainclothesmen wanted to talk to me. Once again, I told them that I didn't have anything to say, but I did ask them what I was doing here in Aichach. They didn't answer, and the conversation ended.

After a few days, one of my lawyers finally arrived and told me why I had been moved. I was to appear at a police lineup for the policeman who had checked my papers at the Bremgarten highway carpark and had been shot. For weeks now, the public prosecutor's office had been trying to organize this lineup without my lawyer being present. That was why the custodial judge in Hamburg had not said anything about my transfer beforehand. However, as might be expected, the whole thing was a farce. The policeman was already on record saying that I was the same woman whose ID card had been found in the Volkswagen. As I later learned from the investigation files, the plan was to carry out the lineup in a way that deviated considerably from what was prescribed in the Code of Criminal Procedure. Instead of me standing in line with other women of my height and build, I was to be presented to the policeman alone.

Even before finding this out, I had already decided that I would not voluntarily take part in any of the procedures organized by the courts. I expected neither justice nor fairness. My intention was to draw clear lines. Each day in prison confirmed what my friends from the RAF had been saying in our first conversations in Heidelberg: the state fights against revolutionaries with everything at its disposal, including illegal tactics. Besides, I obviously had no interest whatsoever in actually being identified by the policeman when face to face with him. My papers and my fingerprints in the car were evidence that I had used it. But that didn't necessarily mean I was the woman who had given the policeman her ID card.

After a good week or so, I was told to pack again, and this time they brought me to the men's prison in Freiburg. They put me in the last cell in a row of empty cells at the end of a corridor with a policewoman positioned outside the locked door. It was strange and threatening to be the only woman in a men's prison. I could hear the men's voices and shouts all around.

The next morning, they brought me to a room in the administrative block. Aside from two chairs and a table, it was empty. All day long, they tried various tricks to arrange a "chance meeting" with the injured policeman, fetching me out of the cell under all sorts of pretexts. They led me up and down staircases and along corridors to the toilet; they lied to me, telling me my lawyer was there. When it became clear to me what they were trying to do, I simply refused to leave the room again, even when they said it was to bring me before a judge. So the judge came to me, and with some very reasonable news: "Without the presence of your lawyer, you do not have to take part in any questioning or police lineup organized by the public prosecutor's office."

When my lawyer finally turned up, they also had to bring him to me. And when he lodged a formal complaint about the way the police lineup was to be conducted, they had to admit defeat.

Then Günter Textor appeared in my cell. He was the head of the RAF Special Commission of the Stuttgart State Criminal Police Office (Landeskriminalamt, LKA). This man, who barely came up to my shoulders, pranced in front of me, almost exploding with fury. "You are not yet in power!" he screamed, "You are not yet in a position to do whatever you want!"

They then brought me to Freiburg Railway Station. I couldn't help but think back to the first time I had boarded a train at this long, rectangular building three months before. I had escaped then. It was true that they now had me in their grip, but that didn't mean the struggle was over.

The Special Commission occupied one compartment, with me sitting in the middle of the officers, without handcuffs, so that nobody would know who was travelling with them. Guards were standing in the corridor, and they repeatedly tried to strike up a conversation with me, or at the very least to provoke me into some kind of reaction. They asked me which prison was worse—Hamburg, Freiburg, or Aichach? That was a question I could have answered, but I remained silent.

In Hamburg, the police cleared the section of the station where our train was arriving. A police car drove right up onto the platform to pick me up, and, once again, as on the journey from Hamburg, we drove through the streets in a convoy with blue lights flashing, through red lights all the way to Holstenglacis prison. It was well into the evening and, when the police car drove into the yard of the men's prison under all the floodlights, hundreds of prisoners roared and banged on their windows to greet me, making a huge racket.

I was totally exhausted from the journey, the massive surveillance, the prison transfers, and the constant effort I had had to make to avoid falling into the police's traps. I had summoned up all my strength, and I had survived every situation as I had planned. Back in Hamburg, where I knew my way around, I broke down at something quite ridiculous. I had asked for a cup of coffee, which I only liked with milk, and when I was told there wasn't any milk left, it was all too much. During my two-week journey from one prison to another, I had drunk whatever happened to be there. Typical watery prison coffee that looked and tasted like dishwater. Or instant coffee without milk. Or water. And now, in familiar surroundings, the lack of milk made me burst into tears. After I had pulled myself together, I was shocked and ashamed of my breakdown.

Learning in Prison and the May Offensive

Alone in my cell, I spent a lot of time thinking about my family and my childhood and adolescence.

The main things that had pushed me to go from the Release to the SPK and then to the RAF had to do with the way I felt about life at the time, with what I had experienced within my family, at school, and in society. I had never been able to find my real self in any of those places. Life just didn't make sense to me. Everywhere I looked, I saw lies, restrictions, violence; I couldn't accept that that was the way things were.

I had been searching for an identity that embodied a sense of political and personal morality, and this search had led me to the RAF.

Now I was locked up in a cell, confronted again and again with these two situations: the shootout at the Bremgarten car park and the shootout in Hamburg. It was like a nightmare that wouldn't leave me be. I jumped every time I heard a bang, and whenever I heard police sirens outside the prison walls I was overcome with fear and a sense of paralysis. "Why didn't you shoot?" Holger had asked. He was right: Why didn't I? Was I incapable of doing so? Would I have been able to in a different situation? I believed that the use of violence was justified, so why hadn't I used violence myself? Was I incapable of taking part in the armed struggle? The actual situation when it happened had completely steamrolled me. The memories of what had happened wouldn't go away. They haunted me, and I was unable to put any distance between myself and what had transpired. The idea that the shootout in Bremgarten had been unnecessary, brutal even, and that I didn't even want to shoot, was something I could not admit to myself. I also couldn't admit to myself that I had been the wrong person to accompany Ulrike that evening.

I decided to use my time in prison for learning. As it took some time before the custodial judge allowed me to order any books, Heinemann, the director of the women's section of the Hamburg prison, offered to bring me books she had at home or from the prison library. She asked me what sort of books I wanted. Heinemann didn't at all fit my image of a prison director. She was friendly, informed me about judicial procedures, and tried to implement the ideas of prison being a place for rehabilitation.

I asked her for books about the Nazi period, which I wanted to learn more about. Until my release from prison in February 1973, the history of twentieth century Germany remained a central theme in my studies, from the Weimar Republic to the Nazi era, right up to the founding of the Federal Republic of Germany and the postwar period. First, I read everything I could get my hands on about Hitler's fascism: academic books from the US and the USSR, biographies of reactionaries, Social Democrats, and communists, as well as fiction.

When I was at school, our history lessons had stopped at World War I, and my parents remained silent whenever we children asked questions about the Nazi period and World War II. I had always suspected that important things had happened in their lives during that period, but that it was something we weren't supposed to talk about. "We couldn't do anything about what Hitler did," was all we heard. "We didn't know what was going on."

My mother was twenty-one at the end of the war, my father thirty-two. They hadn't been members of any National Socialist Party organization, but they had identified with the Nazi ideology. With the military liberation from fascism on May 8, 1945, their world fell apart, both their material situation and everything they believed in.

It was my father's dream as a young man to study music, but his father had forbidden him from doing so, because he did not consider being a musician a respectable profession. So my father began studying to be a teacher, which he abandoned during the war and, after being disappointed in love, he volunteered to go to the front. The Soviet victory at the Battle of Stalingrad caused a decisive rupture in his life. His self-confidence and his worldview were shattered forever. When he became a professional soldier in the new West German army, the Bundeswehr, in 1957, he was able to pick up where he had left off in 1945 when everything had fallen apart for him. He worked without passion at the Cologne headquarters of the MAD, drowning his memories in alcohol.

My mother was the first to apply to visit, but I didn't want to see her. She wrote me letters that I didn't answer. My parents had assisted the police in their manhunt and had talked about me to the press. That confirmed my opinion of them and reinforced my contempt. The world they lived in was now more distant than ever; we had nothing in common. Despite everything, this hurt me, and I cried when I read my mother's letters, which were replete with angst, threats, and emotional blackmail. I was envious of others who had understanding and supportive parents, but I didn't feel it would be possible for us to build any bridges. The nature of my mother's love for me was such that she would have followed me across the world, just to find me and lock me up at home. My father would have never bothered looking for me, but would nonetheless have also locked me up at home if he could.

I also received letters from friends from school in Bonn or from when I attended university, as well as from my ex-boyfriend and his wife. Other political prisoners wrote to me too. The first one was Werner Hoppe, who was incarcerated on the other side of the prison in the men's block. He had been in a car with Petra Schelm when they had run into a police roadblock on June 15, 1971. Petra had been shot dead, and he had been arrested. Werner wrote to me as if we had always known one another, even though I had never met him. He wrote me very emotional letters, called me his "sister, friend, comrade," sent me a thousand hugs in his thoughts, and provided the first words of advice to help me come to terms with my new situation as a prisoner in isolation. He said I should exercise regularly to stay fit, both physically and mentally. I started immediately and, in all the years I spent in jail, I didn't miss a single day. He wrote down poems by Bertolt Brecht, wrote about communism in the Weimar Republic, about Erich Mühsam and Max Hölz. He recommended books, and even sent me two or three before doing so was forbidden. He too had read a lot about fascism and the Weimar Republic, and so we were able to share our thoughts and questions in our letters. The closeness and the warmth he managed to create between us helped me a great deal, and I felt that we were often thinking and feeling similar things. One comrade on the outside who wrote to both of us told me later, "I was always fascinated when I received letters from either of you. Although they were written separately and independent of one another, they often contained almost identical thoughts and feelings. This is a phenomenon I also experienced with other prisoners from the RAF."

The men's block where Werner was housed also contained the sick bay where the women had to be taken when they needed a doctor. One day I wanted to go to the doctor and extensive preparations were made, because to get there I had to go through the men's block. As other prisoners weren't allowed to see me, all of the prisoners whose cells were in the corridors I had to go through were locked up before I started off. I had gone through almost the entire building accompanied by several prison guards and minders, when, around a corner up ahead, there suddenly appeared a similar group with a prisoner in handcuffs. Prior to that moment, I had never seen Werner, who, at the time, was the only other RAF prisoner apart from me at the Hamburg prison. Yet we immediately realized what was going on and flung ourselves at each other, managing to hug before the surprised guards could tear us apart.

In its attempt to plan every step down to the smallest detail, the bloated security apparatus had tied itself in knots and had brought about exactly what it had been aiming to avoid: an encounter between two enemies of the state. I drew a great deal of strength from this meeting; I was able to draw sustenance from it for months afterward, and it reduced the impact of the many indignities inflicted upon me. It was a feeling of gratification at the failure of the prison and security apparatus, as well as a feeling like having met another human being in a desert.

I organized my life in prison according to a daily schedule: at least one hour of exercise, followed by a study of difficult texts after breakfast. These included classics from the workers' movement, such as Marx, Engels, Lenin, Lukács, Rosa Luxemburg, or more recent theorists from France, Italy, Germany, and the US, as well as reports from the Third World. At midday, I listened to an hour of news on the radio, while the afternoon was set aside for letter-writing. After that I read newspapers and, in between, autobiographies and novels. At 7:00 p.m., another hour of news on the radio and, after that, maybe a feature story about the Third World.

Some of the female guards made no secret of their dislike for me. Others kept a certain distance or were even friendly. One of them came to see me—in secret, as the guards were not allowed to be alone with me in my cell—and bombarded me with questions. She wanted to know what we were fighting for, what we wanted to change, what my family was like, and why I refused to see them. She brought me fruit and other treats. Her visits did not go unnoticed, and she was soon transferred to another prison. She gave me her watch as a going away present. Another guard would sometimes open my door for just a second, slipping me a note asking if there was anything I needed. She never spoke to me, so she was never found out.

It was the beginning of a new era for me, a time marked by a very special kind of interaction with other people, unlike anything I had experienced before: I not only corresponded with other prisoners, but a great deal of mail also arrived for me from different parts of West Germany, from people who were members of political groups I had never heard of. They told me about their work, sent me their political pamphlets and newspapers, and wanted to know what I thought. I participated in their discussions from my cell, and my thoughts and ideas were listened to and taken seriously.

I was allowed one half-hour visit every fourteen days; people I had never met before came, and we got on well from the get-go. I wrote letters to Stefan from Hamburg on a weekly basis, and he visited me regularly. He was an apprentice and trade union activist from the Proletarian Front (Proletarische Front, PF), yet he still found time to read and write. He was searching for something different, and the armed struggle seemed like a realistic choice, which is why he wrote to me. Christiane from Frankfurt was active in the women's group of Revolutionary Struggle (Revolutionärer Kampf, RK). She was studying to become a teacher, was involved in squatting activities, and worked in a grassroots group in the district she lived in. As she lived in Frankfurt, she couldn't visit me very often, but we wrote each other every month. She was disgusted at the way I had been dragged before the press after my arrest and about my prison conditions, and this is what first prompted her to write. She had her doubts about whether the armed struggle made sense.

Christiane, Stefan, and I all enjoyed a special relationship, feeling we were on the same side fighting against the same enemy: against the state machine, against imperialism. And the situation in which we got to know each other made for a particularly intense kind of relationship. Every letter was gone over by a judge, and a copy was made for the district attorney's office. Our visits took place in a cell in the middle of the women's prison that had been completely emptied, save for a table and four chairs. We had to sit at opposite ends of the table with a female guard and somebody from State Security seated right behind us, listening to everything we said, constantly taking notes. In situations like this, it took a great deal of concentration for me to keep my thoughts together.

On March 2, 1972, I was lying on my bed as usual, listening to the hourly news on the radio. "During a police control today in Augsburg," I heard the news anchor say, "twenty-three-year old Thomas Weisbecker was shot and killed, and the woman accompanying him, Carmen Roll, twenty-four years of age, was arrested."

The news took my breath away. I had met Tommy once when he was at the flat in Hamburg where we forged passports, shortly before I was arrested. I clenched my fists and cried. The third death on our side in such a short span of time: Petra Schelm, Georg von Rauch, and now Tommy. And I couldn't do a thing. I was locked up in this hole, enraged but also full of fear. The same could have happened to me. When Georg was shot, I was freezing in Aichach; I learned of his death from the broadcasts on the prison speakers, but at the time I hadn't actually grasped what had happened, because I was so involved in my own situation, waiting to be attacked at any moment. Now, I had to think about him too.

I knew Carmen from the SPK, and she had also been in Hamburg before my arrest. She was the only one who had made any attempt to reach out to me in my loneliness and

despair and to let me know that she understood what I was
going through. Now she was in Aichach. I could well imagine how she felt in that medieval tomb, and I wrote to her
immediately. They had given her a general anesthetic in her
cell in order to take her fingerprints and had nearly killed
her in the process. This was a horrific act; her lawyers and
family protested against a resisting prisoner being given a
general anesthetic to make the police's forensic work easier,
under conditions that did not allow for any kind of emergency care. However, as nobody had had to witness such a
scene on television, the public reaction was minimal.

My brother Dieter visited me two or three times. He was
unhappy with his studies in business economics, a really
dry subject, and dissatisfied with his life and looked to me
to give him some kind of direction, his big sister who had
often also been a substitute mother for him. He wanted to
know what the prison conditions were like and how I was
coping, what I was thinking, and why I had taken the steps
that had landed me in prison.

We tried to reminisce about how we had lived when we
were kids in a temporary run-down housing estate outside
of Oberursel near Frankfurt. My parents had been uprooted
by the war. My mother's family had fled from Pomerania,
and, even if he had wanted to, my father would not have
been able to live with his family in Frankfurt following his
return. After what he had experienced, he no longer felt he
would be able to become a teacher, so he took on a job as a
gardener with an aging relative of my mother's who was a
bit of an oddball. His work was on the outskirts of Oberursel
where the barracks were. In this oppressive place of poverty,
violence, and despair, our parents drummed into us that we
were different from the other children in the housing estate,
that we were better and should keep our distance from them.
Our father had a violent temper, was dissatisfied with life,
taciturn, and, like all the other fathers on the estate, he didn't

know what he had done to deserve such a life. At night, our mother worked at home sewing sparkling beads onto fabrics, because what my father earned wasn't enough. She hated domestic chores and would often crawl into bed with poetry books, leaving me to look after my siblings and do the house-work, despite my very young age.

In later years, when I went to grammar school, the tables were turned: all of a sudden, I was the one who came from that housing estate for the displaced, who had no nice clothes and no money for anything. School was a nightmare for me.

We recalled moving to Bonn in 1958 and living in a new housing estate—one block of flats after another. The neigh-bors hardly knew each other, and the families who lived there seldomly got on well with one another. You could hear every radio, every loud word, and you knew who was hit-ting whom and when. A family with ten children lived in the block behind us in a flat with three tiny rooms. The man was Catholic, and his wife was pregnant every year, becom-ing more and more desperate with each pregnancy. When she was expecting her eleventh child, she went out one day and threw herself in front of a train. A short time after her death, her husband married a young woman to be mother to his ten children.

I told Dieter about what I had come across while reading memoirs and novels from and about the Nazi period. During our childhood and when we were teenagers, we often made music. All three of us children learned piano and recorder, and we sang together. I now discovered that much of this music came directly from the Nazi repertoire or had been used by the Nazis. Realizing this was such a shock to me that I never wanted to sing a German carol again. All at once, it became clear to me how the Nazis had taken possession of an important part of German culture. They had used Schiller and Goethe just like they had used the traditional folk songs, to celebrate their "blood and soil" ideology.

We spoke about the violence we had experienced, and on this issue we understood one another. However, I couldn't tell him what to do with his life now, as the chasm between his world in Bonn and my world was too great. I didn't hear anything from him for some time, and then I received a letter from my mother telling me that my brother was catatonic, and she had had to commit him to a psychiatric institution. She also said that she was thinking of committing suicide, and that it was all my fault. It took every ounce of strength that I had not to let myself be talked into feeling guilty by all these pleas and accusations, to stop myself from being caught up in the old patterns of guilt and remorse.

I threw myself into studying and reading, very curious to find out what this new world I was entering was like and in what direction things were going to go. I began to better understand the new dimension of the struggle—internationalism—which my friends from the RAF had had a considerable effect on when they had decided to engage in armed struggle. For the first time, I read books about the war in Vietnam, about the fight against the Shah in Iran, the struggles for freedom in Africa, and the guerrillas in Latin America. I learned about the Tupamaros in Uruguay and FRELIMO and Amilcar Cabral in Africa. I began to see where the vast amounts of wealth in West Germany, the rest of Europe, and the US came from and what crimes had been committed by imperialism around the world.

When I read about the crimes of the American military in Vietnam, a deep hate welled up in me, looking for an outlet and an opportunity to turn ideas into practice. I read how the US planes and ships that waged war against the people of Vietnam took off from German soil and embarked from German ports. It was in books that I learned how German money and German companies together with North American, French, and British companies were destroying the Third World and plundering the populations there so that the ruling class in Europe and the US could get richer and richer. This further convinced me that armed struggle, even in West Germany, was right and justified.

I felt a strong sympathy and solidarity for the freedom fighters from the national liberation movements on all continents. When I read texts by Iranian, African, or Latin American guerrilla fighters, it seemed to me that we were speaking the same language. We had the same enemy worldwide: the agents and shareholders of colonialism and imperialism. "You are fighting in the heart of the beast," Che had said to those fighting in Europe and the US.

The Wretched of the Earth by Frantz Fanon, a book about the experiences of those involved in the Algerian freedom struggle against French colonial power, and its foreword by Jean-Paul Sartre, reinforced my conviction that I was fighting on the right side for the right cause, using the necessary means. I didn't want objective disinterested theories. I passionately took the side of the poor and downtrodden who were fighting for their rights.

And as there were so few of us in Germany, even in Europe, and the crimes were so immense, the only legitimate instrument was counterviolence. It seemed naive, blind, and nonsensical to me to hope to fight against the violence of governments, armies, and large corporations using non-violent means. Technological advances meant that violence in the Third World was being fine-tuned and was becoming institutionalized. The hunger there was the flipside to our obscene wealth here. The presumptuousness and arrogance were endlessly violent. The weapons, the orders, and often the soldiers fighting the wars on the continents where there was so much misery came from the metropoles of the developed world.

In the 1950s, a movement had started to put an end to colonialism: liberation movements and national liberation struggles in the Third World organized themselves and fought for their independence from the old European colonial powers and the US.

In the 1970s, this led to a change in the international balance of power. European and North American imperialism could no longer simply do what it wanted in the Third World—the largest part of the world. There were liberated territories and liberation movements. At the time, we couldn't imagine how quickly and how absolutely the national independence movements would reach their limits, but we understood that no region in the Third World could gain and maintain its freedom if the economic and military power of the metropoles, of Europe and the US, remained secure. We—and we were not alone—were convinced that it was possible to disrupt these metropoles and interfere with their ability to function. Was there not a historic opportunity here for worldwide revolution?

When and where was it legitimate to use violence? Many on the left said it was justified for the liberation movements in the Third World to engage in armed struggle, but not in Europe, where democracy ruled. But what kind of a democracy was it that only functioned internally and didn't apply to the outside world? Were the people in the Third World a less valuable class of human being? Is violence always and only legitimate when perpetrated by the state?

These questions preoccupied me, and in examining them I was seeking to find a different morality for myself, a different path in life. One thing was clear: if you decide to act, you have to be willing to get your hands dirty, and you must accept responsibility, no matter what. Given the choice between looking on as a mere bystander or acting, there was no hesitation. I had to opt for the latter, despite any mistakes that might be made. I wanted to do my part to make sure that those responsible for so much suffering would not be able to sleep soundly while their weapons killed people in other parts of the world.

Then the RAF's May Offensive happened.

On May 11, 1972, three bombs exploded in the head-quarters of the 5th US Army Corps in Frankfurt, killing one officer. On May 12, bombs exploded at the police head-quarters in both Augsburg and Munich. On May 15, a bomb exploded under the car belonging to Federal Judge Wolfgang Buddenberg, who was responsible for imposing isolation conditions on political prisoners. The bomb injured his wife who was the one in the car when it went off. On May 19, a blast went off in the Hamburg offices of the Springer Corporation. A warning issued beforehand had been ignored, and several employees were injured. On May 24, in Heidelberg, bombs exploded in the US Army's European headquarters; three soldiers died.

There was no end to it. I had difficulty following it all and thinking through what was happening. Had I envisioned these kinds of actions when I had decided, while reading in my cell, that the armed struggle was correct? Would I myself have taken part in organizing them? Four US soldiers had been killed in the attacks on the US military bases in Heidelberg and Frankfurt. The war against Vietnam was being fought from those bases. The military airplanes and soldiers flew out from there, and from there they planned the missions for bomb attacks, arrests, torture, and the arbitrary murder of the elderly, women, children, and the Viet Cong. I felt that any means to stop all of that were justified. However, I couldn't rejoice in what had happened, because I felt that I was incapable of using violence myself.

The West German government responded to the May Offensive with the biggest manhunt in the history of the Federal Republic, bringing all traffic in the country to a stand-still for an entire day. The US government sent in counterin-surgency "specialists." At the end of May, there was a bomb threat, supposedly from the RAF, stating that several bombs would go off on June 2 in the busy Stuttgart city center, so that the people of that city could experience first hand what the people in Hanoi had to put up with during US bombardments. I thought, "The RAF would never do anything like that." In my apartment in Heidelberg, my friends had talked about how activities had to be directed against those responsible; while this might include those tasked with protecting them, it should never be directed against the population at large. Why would something like this happen now? All my senses switched to alarm mode. The RAF immediately issued a statement, specifying that they had nothing to do with these threats: "The fake communiqués, given their contents, their purpose, their essence, and their style, more likely come from the cops themselves." However, this statement was never made public.

Andreas Baader, Holger Meins, and Jan-Carl Raspe were captured on June 1, Gudrun Ensslin on June 7, Ulrike Meinhof and Gerhard Müller on June 15, Brigitte Mohnhaupt and Bernhard Braun on June 20, and, on July 8, Irmgard Möller and Klaus Jünschke.

With this wave of arrests, all of the founding members of the RAF had been captured. Was this the end, or were there other RAF comrades I didn't know who would continue the struggle?

Immediately after being arrested, Ulrike was sent to the Dead Wing in Cologne-Ossendorf, where Astrid Proll had been up to that point. This was an empty whitewashed medical wing separate from the other prison buildings. Ulrike saw no other prisoners and heard nobody but the prison guards. Acoustic isolation. Sensory deprivation. White torture. She described later in a letter: "The feeling, one's head explodes … the feeling, the cell moves … . One cannot tell whether one shivers from fever or from cold—one cannot tell why one shivers—one freezes. To speak at a normal volume requires an effort like that necessary to speak loudly, almost like that necessary to shout—the feeling, one falls silent—one can no longer identify the meaning of words, one can only guess ... headaches ... . When writing: two lines—by the end of the second line, one cannot remember the beginning of the first—The feeling, internal burnout." And in another letter, "[I]n the absolute, absolutely perceivable silence, the entire force of resistance does not have any object, other than oneself. As you cannot fight the silence, you can only fight what is happening with yourself, to yourself, that is, you end up only fighting yourself. That is the aim of the Dead Wing: to achieve the self-destruction of the prisoners."

Drawing on the few pieces of information about the Dead Wing published by the lawyers in those first weeks, I tried to imagine Ulrike's situation. My isolation in Hamburg was different. I wasn't allowed to be with the other prisoners, but I could hear them and see them and I took part in their lives indirectly. In the evenings, I had long conversations with them from window to window, and sometimes one of them even managed to swing something over to me on a piece of string: a page out of a newspaper, a cigarette, something sweet. In this way, I found out why one woman screamed, cried, and ranted for hours in her cell. After considering the evidence against her for three hours, the court had sentenced her to ten years. After years of desperation and indignity, she had stabbed her husband, who had beaten her and her children whenever he got drunk. The children were placed in a home. The legal counsel assigned by the court, whom she met for the first time at her trial, did not file a single motion on her behalf.

This was not an isolated case. There were three women in the small women's prison in Hamburg who had similar stories and who had also been sentenced to ten years by the Hamburg courts. I passed on the address of my lawyer Kurt Groenewold to one of the women via one of the guards who was willing to do favors like that, so that he could at least help at her appeal and maybe even win a retrial. Kurt was a dedicated lawyer who often visited me while I was in prison, helping me at difficult times.

In September 1972, the Palestinian Black September commando unit attacked the Israeli team's accommodations at the Munich Olympic Games, killing two athletes and taking nine Israelis hostage. The commando demanded the release of two hundred Arab prisoners incarcerated in Israel. The police attempted to free the hostages at the Fürstenfeldbruck airport, which resulted in a bloodbath. All nine Israelis, five guerrillas, and one policeman were killed, and this was shown live on television to a worldwide audience. I didn't have a TV, but I followed the whole thing on the radio. I was shocked at the intensity of the confrontation, and I didn't understand the reason for it. This event encouraged me to learn more about the creation of the State of Israel and the brutal expulsion of the Palestinians from their own country. I was outraged by what I learned, and my sympathies lay with the Palestinian liberation struggle.

On October 20, another Palestinian commando unit skyjacked a Lufthansa plane and demanded the release of the three surviving members of the commando unit that had carried out the Munich hostage-taking. This ended without bloodshed when the three Palestinians were allowed to fly out of the country.

First Trial

My first trial date was approaching.

The custodial judge was replaced by a criminal judge, and there were several changes to my prison conditions. People who had been refused previously were now allowed to visit, even friends from the former SPK. We were really happy to see one another and spent the visits laughing about all sorts of things, despite the fact that my situation wasn't funny at all—stuck in a tiny cell in the middle of the prison, with State Security officers following my every move and listening to every word, no matter how insignificant. One time, two of my friends were able to come at the same time, and we had a ball: for a short time, it almost felt like we were on the outside.

My isolation was relaxed a little within the prison. First, I was allowed to watch television with other prisoners for two hours once a week, though I had to sit on the outside with a guard right next to me. Later, I was allowed to spend my half hour in the yard, my so-called "free time," with the others.

I had often seen a young Turkish woman from my window. She always walked alone, and I found out during my evening window-to-window conversations that she had been charged with murder. She had stabbed her husband. As she had only come to Germany a short time before, she couldn't speak a word of German. From her face, you could see that she cried a lot, yet she emanated a sense of dignity that immediately caught my attention. One day, I approached her during our yard time, and we hit it off right away, doing our best to communicate using fingers, hands, and eyes. I began to teach her a little German, and we were allowed to continue these lessons for one hour a day in an empty cell. This turned out to be quite complicated, because Fatima couldn't write. However, with the help of a German-Turkish dictionary I ordered, she eventually learned to speak and write German, while I learned Turkish.

I also began preparing for my trial. My second defense lawyer was Armin Golzem, the friend of my ex-boyfriend whom I had first met in Frankfurt in 1970. He had a good reputation as a sharp-tongued criminal defense lawyer in political trials, always ready to uncover inconsistencies in the evidence and to go on the attack.

I was given access to my files, five or six thick volumes that I began to study page by page. I wanted to know what the Office of the Federal Prosecutor knew, and I looked for discrepancies and errors to point out to the lawyers. We discussed what motions to file and what strategy we wanted to pursue at trial.

In early 1972, the Office of the Federal Prosecutor had withdrawn the charges for murder and attempted murder. I felt this was irrelevant, however, as I assumed they would still find some way of sentencing me to ten years or more.

The charges against me were aiding and abetting a criminal organization pursuant to Paragraph 129, possession of a weapon without a permit, forging documents, and aiding and abetting attempted murder (at the shootout at the Bremgarten motorway car park).

I was certain of one thing—I was not going to make any statements about the charges. I assumed that at the judicial level the judges and the public prosecutors had the power to do whatever they wanted, and that they would proceed based on ideological and political criteria. Justice was class justice. I wanted to show what I thought about this justice by the way I conducted myself at trial: given its Nazi traditions and practices, I did not recognize its legitimacy or its right to convict me. No judge from the Nazi period was ever convicted—many of them remained at their posts—and Paragraph 129, which was being used to prosecute me, dated back to before Hitler.

I prepared a statement to read at the trial. When I was finished, I sent it via my lawyer to other prisoners from the RAF, wanting to know what they thought. "The statement is shit, completely apolitical," was Andreas's reaction. "Leave her alone," Gudrun said, "that's what she's like." Horst Mahler suggested a few changes. I didn't hear from anyone else.

The trial began on November 15, 1972, not at the court directly next to the prison but in Hamburg-Wandsbek. State Security considered that to be safer and had built an annex to the court building especially for the occasion. They took me there on the morning of the trial, accompanied by an enormous police presence. I was tense and nervous as I entered the courtroom, which was full of reporters and other people, most of whom I didn't know. Many greeted me with their fists raised in salute and with expressions of sympathy. Being in a room full of people was a real shock to me after so much time spent alone, but it also gave me strength. While the lawyers and the court—a jury court with three professional judges and lay judges—engaged in a legal skirmish about the trial being relocated to Wandsbek and access restrictions for trial observers, I took a look at who was in the room with me. Several people gave me furtive signs of solidarity; some had brought flowers. Then I read my first trial statement:

> Four months ago, my brother Werner Hoppe was sentenced to ten years isolation and forced labor. After thirty-three "days on trial," violence was declared law. This "explosive conviction," as it was called in the liberal press, made perfectly clear that the abstract constitutional state and a court that is a loyal state servant

are two different things. Judge Schmidt's nightmare formed the basis of his decision. What is significant here is that these "explosives" are being planted in every courtroom every day so inconspicuously that when they go off it looks like an occupational hazard. Whoever puts their hand into the machinery is always to blame. Guilty is he who cannot react differently to the violence that destroys him daily, who cannot react other than to direct this violence toward himself, to pass it on subconsciously and sporadically, or to fight back. On at least four occasions this year, Judge Schmidt caused such an explosion in the prison where I have been incarcerated for thirteen months, an explosion that erased ten years of a human being's life ...

My solidarity, the solidarity of the revolutionary intellectuals with those who are exploited, oppressed, their lives rendered unlivable, comes from being aware that life in our society is only possible at the cost of the ill, the oppressed, and the exploited; that every one of us is a part of the violence and oppression, and there is no way out for us. Everyone in our society embodies the conflict of either being an instrument of authority or being controlled and oppressed himself. This means, he has to decide! ... The only weapon against the violence of the authorities is the violence and the solidarity of the oppressed! ...

If you reject violence, if you really hate it—and I hate violence!—then all that is left is to do everything you can to get rid of this hated violence. The violence that prevails is the violence of inhumanity and oppression, violence against it is violence against inhumanity and oppression, that is, humane and liberating violence. We have to fight against and overcome our acquired paralyzing fear of using violence ourselves; we are the only ones suffering from this paralysis, it does not affect capital or its protectors …

After that, we went back and forth three times a week, through roadblocks and red lights, me in a police van with both marked and unmarked cars in front and behind.

The court building was sealed off by roughly a hundred police; everyone attending the trial had to show ID.

After thirteen months in isolation, every day at trial was an enormous physical and emotional strain on me, although I did nothing but sit there for hours saying nothing. The presence of so many people, their noises and their smells, having to concentrate on the words of others—I just wasn't used to it anymore, and it took all the strength I had. When I was brought back to my cell in the afternoon or evening, I would fall on my bed trembling from exhaustion, unable to do anything whatsoever. I no longer even managed to read the newspaper.

The days of the trial passed, with witness statements and experts being questioned. The evidence was entered, the lawyers filed applications, and the courts made decisions. A woman I had never seen before appeared as a witness. She explained how she had ended up in the RAF, how she had lived as part of the group, and why she had eventually gone back to her family. She was about my age, and her story reminded me of my own: nobody had forced her to do any-thing when she joined the Berlin RAF comrades. How could she live with herself, now that she had returned to the arms of her family and become a state witness? I could under-stand how somebody might no longer want or be able to continue, but betrayal? To testify against your own friends to save your skin? I could only feel contempt.

I never spoke a word about "the matter" itself, but I issued several statements, mainly about the conditions in Hamburg's prisons, the situation of the political prisoners, and the hype surrounding the trial. There were often disruptions in the spectators' gallery, and the court eventually had supporters barred.

On January 17, 1973, the RAF prisoners began their first hunger strike against isolation, which all of the approximately sixty political prisoners were being subjected to. When I heard the hunger strike had started, I was unsure. Nobody had informed me about it beforehand, and I had never thought about going on hunger strike myself. Should I join in, despite the fact that I was in the middle of a trial? Was a hunger strike dangerous? Could you get sick or die? Were you allowed to take liquids? I had lots of food from my weekly purchases in my cell. What should I do with it? Push it under the bed? Put it outside the cell?

A few minutes after I told my guard that I was going to join in the hunger strike, the prison doctor turned up. She told me that a hunger strike was very dangerous, that I would almost certainly be barred from the trial, and that if I insisted on going on hunger strike I should at least drink lots of tea with sugar. Nothing she told me was true, but I didn't realize that until later. And I would most likely have ruined my health if I had followed her advice and taken sugar.

The prison administration refused to take the box of food out of my cell, so I put it under my bed. I was already suffering from dizziness after the first day, with even worse problems concentrating than before. I felt hungry, and the box was under my bed. I ate a little. After three days battling with myself back and forth, I gave up.

In court, I read out a declaration of solidarity with the hunger strike with the demand to "end isolation" and "transfer Ulrike out of the Dead Wing." Then I tried to have myself excluded from the trial, so that I would no longer have to take part in it. When the court wouldn't exclude me, I began talking loudly and being a nuisance, until the order was given to have me forcibly removed. When that happened, supporters expressed their solidarity in such a way that the whole episode ended in a brawl.

On February 5, 1973, my sentence was pronounced: two years and three months, with imprisonment suspended until the conviction came into force. I was no longer attending the trial, and, in fact, was taking a bath a few days later when a guard hammered on the door, saying, "You're being released Frau Schiller." This wasn't what I had expected. However, as was often the case at critical moments, I remained calm, focusing on what was going to happen next. I quickly dried myself, and they brought me to my cell, where I threw all of my belongings into a plastic bag. Then my lawyers arrived and accompanied me to a side exit.

Journalists were waiting in front of the prison gates snapping pictures and with their TV cameras running. A small group of friends and comrades were also waiting for me, among them the mother of the singer Wolf Biermann, who lived in Hamburg and was friends with my lawyer. We walked in a demonstration with flags flying to a nearby Greek restaurant. One sip of red wine, and I already had a red face and hot cheeks.

I had no idea what I was going to do now.

Freedom

February 9, 1973, the day of my release, was also the start of a three-day solidarity hunger strike by lawyers and family members of the RAF prisoners, who were already themselves on hunger strike. There was a protest on the busy street in front of the Federal Court of Justice, which was where most of the decisions concerning the prison conditions had been made. This strike was one of the first public actions by the prisoners' friends and family members against isolation torture.

I decided to participate. The next day, I took a train to Heidelberg with my lawyer Kurt Groenewold and one of his colleagues. We were picked up at the station by two other lawyers and drove in their car to Karlsruhe. It was already evening, and we talked about the prisoners' situation and about my experiences and those of the lawyers. They told me how the prisoners they knew personally were managing. All of a sudden, in the middle of our conversation, I was dead tired. Why was I falling asleep now, when there were so many new things to hear, smell, and see? With all the strength I could muster, I fought against this inexplicable fatigue and managed to push through it. I looked at my watch and saw that it was exactly 10:00 p.m. For one and a half years, the light had gone out at exactly this time, and this conditioning had followed me into my life on the outside. Prison wasn't finished with me yet.

In Karlsruhe, I had my first meeting with family members who were supporting their siblings and children in prison: Ulrike's sister Wienke, Gudrun's sister Christiane, and Andreas's mother Nina. I also met Gabi there, along with other friends from the former SPK who had visited me in prison. We talked with some very young people who had become interested in the prisoners' situation and the guerrilla struggle. They listened wide-eyed to what an "old timer" like me had to tell them. They lived near the Federal Court of Justice and let the hunger strikers sleep at their place.

During the day, we stood on the street in front of the court holding banners. The lawyers had put on their black robes, and passersby would stop to talk with us. Even when these discussions became heated, I never sensed any kind of aggressive rejection. That would come later.

After this three-day hunger strike, Gabi gave me some money to help me get by during this initial period out of prison. I went to Bonn by train to visit my brother, who was sick, and who I hadn't heard from in a long time. I wanted to find out what had happened to him over the past year and see if I could do anything to help. I went to his apartment, but his roommate told me that he was at his daily group therapy session at a local hospital.

I found him on the grounds of the university clinic, in an open psychiatric unit. He hardly reacted when he saw me; his movements were slow, and his face was blank. He had obviously been given strong sedatives. I asked him if he wanted to see me, and he said he did, but that I would have to wait two hours, as he was not finished his group therapy. In the late afternoon, we took a bus to his place, went shopping for food, and cooked together. I asked him about his therapy and about the past year, and he answered my questions in much more detail and with greater ease than I had expected.

However, the next day, we got into a big fight. When I asked him about his long-time girlfriend and their break-up, he began screaming and ranting so much that I thought he was going to have a complete breakdown. Without meaning to, I had touched a very sore nerve. After that, I couldn't talk to him, afraid of unintentionally provoking him. As there was nobody else I wanted to see in Bonn, I returned to Hamburg, troubled and sad. There, I lived in a small basement apartment in my lawyer's house.

As part of my probation, I had to show up at the local police station in Hamburg once a week. If I wanted to travel anywhere, I had to apply for permission from my probation officer. If he said it was alright to travel, I had to check in at the local police station in the town I was visiting.

In the weeks following my release, the aftereffects of isolation became apparent for the first time. After months of being constantly alone, I was now constantly on edge. I felt a great sense of inner turmoil and had problems sleeping. I still had difficulties concentrating, and writing was simply impossible. The gastritis that had begun in prison became chronic. When I was arrested, my periods had stopped from one day to the next and stayed that way during my entire time in prison—one week after being released, they suddenly started again. My hormones had obviously changed somehow, though, because I was no longer able to take the pill, which I had had no problems with prior to my arrest.

I felt that I had changed without really knowing how, and I noticed that the world outside of prison had also changed in my absence. I had to summon up all of my strength to strike up a new relationship with this new world.

One thing that was really hard for me was my new role as a public figure. My high profile had mainly been "created" by the press and didn't bear any relationship to anything I had actually done. I was no longer able to just go somewhere, join in, and listen. I was now regarded and treated as somebody special. This only served to reinforce the feeling of separation from my new surroundings that had been caused by prison. People recognized me everywhere I went. The housewives with their shopping bags smiled at me in the subway, because they recognized my photo from *Bild* newspaper. People would point at me on the street or stop and say hello. It was always in a friendly way, nobody reacted with hostility toward me.

I traveled to Augsburg to visit Helma. She had first written to me after seeing me forcibly dragged in front of the press in Hamburg, and we had maintained an intense correspondence ever since. She had also visited and sent me birthday and Christmas presents while I was in prison, declaring herself to be my adoptive mother. She lived with her husband and son in Augsburg in a small and very modest apartment. After years of illness, she was almost unable to move and felt very lonely in this conservative town. Our friendship had given her new courage in life. Worried, looking at me through her thick glasses, I could see the unasked question in her eyes: What was I going to do now that I had been released? All I could do was hug her with love.

I also went to visit my former boyfriend, who now lived with his wife in Münster. They had both visited me in prison several times and wanted to help me out. They gave me some money, so that I had time to get my bearings.

Every step of the way, no matter where I traveled, I had "company." One time, when I went to Heidelberg, the surveillance by the Baden-Württemberg Special Commission was so over the top that it was intimidating. They drove their car behind me right through a pedestrian area, ostentatiously following me everywhere I went. One night, when Gabi and I were leaving my apartment, where we had met up with some old friends and former members of the SPK, the first thing we did was try to locate the surveillance car on the street. It was nowhere to be seen. "Come on, let's find where they're parked," I said to Gabi. At the next street corner, tucked into a parking space, we discovered one of the cars that often followed us. We ducked down, crept along the sides of the houses, and sneaked up to the parked car. We didn't stand up until we were right next to the car: two police officers were lying on the front seats, which they had reclined. Our sudden appearance at the windows scared the hell out of them. Terrified, they jumped up and pressed the locks down so that we couldn't open the doors from outside and started up the engine, revving it all the way. Gabi and I stood there completely stunned by their reaction: they were afraid of us.

In Hamburg, surveillance by the Special Commission's taskforce was far more discreet, but I soon became skilled at spotting who among the crowds of people and the vehicles around me was following and watching. I learned fast and noticed that I was developing a sixth sense for it; cars or people who crossed your path more than once, eyes that seemed to be searching for nothing in particular, movements that circled around me or that were drawn toward me.

Being in prison, and especially in isolation, gives rise to a strong need for human warmth and tenderness. In my last weeks in prison, I fell in love with Kay. He visited when I was inside and after my release he acted as my bridge between life on the inside and the outside. Kay was younger than me and did not have a lot of political experience. I got to know his circle of friends, all of whom were young and interested in politics but turned off by the hierarchical and rigidly structured Marxist-Leninist groups that had emerged on the left at that time.

My arrest and imprisonment had given me an opportunity to go through and quickly catch up with the political steps I had missed. I thought I might be able to join one of the political groups that I had learned about while in my cell.

In April 1973, there was a meeting in Frankfurt of lawyers, left-wing intellectuals, ex-prisoners, relatives, and visitors of political prisoners, with a plan to set up a defense committee. The idea came from Andreas, Gudrun, and Ulrike, who had written a paper proposing it. At the meeting, there were heated debates over the term "political prisoner." Was it a term that divided the prisoners, or did it apply to those who had become criminals out of political conviction? I was against using the term "political prisoner," as it seemed to set them apart from the other prisoners. Later on, I would understand that division does not come about by simply describing differences for what they are. In the days after this meeting in Frankfurt, I was sharply criticized by Andreas: "What were you thinking, holding up and confusing the whole meeting just because you haven't got a clue about what's what. Shut your mouth and educate yourself before you open it again!"

At the time, besides several smaller groups, there were two larger political organizations that remained separate from the new dogmatic parties: Proletarian Front in Hamburg, with Karl Heinz Roth, and, in Frankfurt, the Revolutionary Struggle group around Daniel Cohn-Bendit and Joschka Fischer. I had read the newspapers of both groups, and Stefan and Christiane, with whom I had corresponded, were members.

The first time I went to a Proletarian Front event in Hamburg, it was an open meeting, and Karl Heinz Roth started it by introducing me and asking me to speak, something I hadn't expected or prepared for. Surprised, I felt out of my depth. I didn't have any experience at public speaking and, as I had come to listen, I turned his offer down.

I often saw Karl Heinz after that. We discussed the dockworkers' situation, because the Proletarian Front carried out a lot of political work among them. While in prison, I had corresponded with a dockworker who had written to me after I was arrested. My talks with Karl Heinz were important to me, because he knew a great deal, and he was also interested in finding out more about me. He was a practicing doctor, wrote political books, and had an enormous capacity to work. He was an intellectual who wanted to put his ideas into practice.

A few weeks after I was released, a message made its way to me, having passed through many hands. Someone from the RAF wanted to see me, instructing me to shake off my followers and to make absolutely sure I wasn't being tailed. The message confused me. I had somehow thought that the RAF had ceased to exist after the 1972 arrests. Who was left, and what could they want from me? I hadn't reckoned with being asked to attend a meeting. However, I didn't hesitate to say yes. No matter who they were or what they wanted from me, they were my comrades.

I got together with Kay, and we mulled over a map of the city and came up with a plan. Setting off several hours before the specified time, we drove around aimlessly in a borrowed car, in order to spot and then lose whatever cars were following us. I put on make-up and, at a place where they could not see us clearly, I suddenly got out and, pulling on a coat and headscarf, ran through a gap in a fence to get onto the city train whose arrival we had checked beforehand on the timetable. From the city train, I transferred to the subway, and then onto several buses, all according to a well-organized schedule. I couldn't hang around anywhere and I had to move fast, changing from one train to another or to a bus.

At the agreed upon meeting point in a small town near Hamburg, I sat down at a table in a pizzeria. Ten minutes later, a tall, thin, black-haired man with a mustache and sunglasses came and sat down next to me. The French newspaper *Le Monde* was the sign we had agreed upon. He flashed me a smile and took off his glasses. I didn't know him. He wanted to know what prison had been like for me, what I knew about how the other prisoners were doing, and what I thought about the political situation on the outside. He said I might meet people who were interested in joining the RAF and, if so, I should put them in touch. He also asked if I wanted to meet with him from time to time. He was obviously tired and nervous. He often glanced over at the other tables and outside the window to see if we were being watched. After about an hour we went our separate ways.

In Hamburg, a colorful mix of young people were squatting a vacant house on Eckhofstraße. The squatters, who included friends of Kay's, wanted to turn it into a youth center, but the police quickly and brutally cleared it out. The ham-fisted reaction of the police and the Hamburg Senate led to the radicalization of many of the young people involved, some of whom would later join the RAF.

Having become acquainted with the Proletarian Front in Hamburg, I also wanted to check out the Revolutionary Struggle group in Frankfurt. When I got there, Daniel Cohn-Bendit invited me to stay at his place; I accepted his offer, staying a few days. He lived with Joschka Fischer and others in a large apartment in an old building. I breakfasted with them and in the evenings we went from pub to pub. It was difficult to talk seriously about anything with Cohn-Bendit, because he put on a little show for everyone who came by to say hello. He didn't completely reject the idea of armed struggle in West Germany, but he was more interested in discussing the when and how. Joschka Fischer was absolutely opposed to violence. Cohn-Bendit's girlfriend was more interested in talking to me about his macho behavior and her never-ending battle against it. She felt that he didn't take her seriously, that he had the important discussions with men, and that she was just there to go to bed with and to look after him, even though she was also active in the group.

I got to know several people in Revolutionary Struggle: from the Opel workers' group, which consisted of left-wing activists and intellectuals who took jobs in the Opel car factory to establish connections to ordinary workers, as well as from the women's group, one of whom had written to me in prison. I also took part in discussions about the squatting activities. The question was whether or not militant means should be used to defend the squats and if the squatters should provoke confrontations with the police. Shortly before, there had been street fights to defend a squat and very different opinions about what to do were being voiced in the evening plenary meetings: Should they hold back, not squatting any new houses, use passive defense, or go on the offensive and defend the houses militantly, while also continuing to look for new houses to squat? How would the city council and the police react?

It was a time of major conflicts, struggles between the left groups over which direction to take, as well as power struggles within the left. What was the best way forward, and who should one join forces with? Was there any chance of success in fighting for the squats? Should leftists go into the factories to the "real" proletariat? Was there a future for revolutionary organization among the dockworkers in Hamburg? How significant was the women's struggle for our organization?

What I often experienced when I got together with people on the left was reflected in a small encounter that I will never forget. In Frankfurt, a woman from Revolutionary Struggle whom I had never met before came into the apartment one day. There was a poster on the wall with my photo on it. When the woman suddenly came upon me in her apartment, in the flesh, she was really upset. In reality, she didn't actually want to be that close to the "politics" with which she adorned her walls. I quickly forgot the conversation we had.

Members of left-wing groups often treated me like an exotic being. I hadn't noticed, but the mythologization of the RAF had already begun. I was the "revolutionary" before my time, someone who had had "real" experiences, because I had been one of the first political prisoners. But not many of them were really interested in what someone like me had to say. It was far more common for people to be afraid and to take a step back, distancing themselves from the guerrilla.

I realized that the arrests of the RAF's founding members, the denunciations of those involved and of the guerrilla's ideas, and the conditions of isolation torture in prison had all left their mark. People were afraid. It had become clear to everyone that revolutionary struggle could have personal consequences, up to and including death.

For many on the left, the guerrilla strategy was a dead end, a failed undertaking. With the arrests of the RAF founders, there was nobody left to carry on the fight. Fear was breathing down people's necks. Was the state too powerful to overcome? The RAF had sought out a confrontation and had seemingly been defeated. Was the concept itself therefore incorrect, or was something wrong with the way it had been put into practice?

In the guerrilla's first years, many people, and not only leftists, had felt a great deal of respect and even awe for those who had begun to fight against the state apparatus, those who had dared to go beyond analysis and mere talk toward practice, risking their own lives in the process. I was also treated with this respect and awe; however, in contrast to the situation in 1970–1972, almost nobody imagined themselves joining the guerrilla struggle.

I saw things differently. Despite my time in prison, I wasn't afraid of the consequences. The way I saw it, the armed struggle had only just begun, and the RAF had not been around nearly long enough to know whether or not the urban guerrilla concept might succeed in the capitalist metropoles. It was clear to me that I lacked political experience, and that the armed struggle would require a high level of specialized skills, knowledge, and political consciousness. But who else would carry out a revolutionary struggle in the Federal Republic of Germany? Was it not true that the majority of workers had become a labor aristocracy that also profited from the exploitation of the Third World? What interest could they possibly have in the destruction of the imperialist system that guaranteed them a standard of living that was built upon the colonization of vast continents? Who in Germany cared about the wars, massacres, torture, and poverty in Asia, Africa, and Latin America? Who was responsible for this?

In early April 1973, Helmut Pohl was released from prison. Wanting to meet him, I phoned his mother in Frankfurt. "It's good that you called," she said. "He really wants to see you." I took the next train to Frankfurt. Helmut was waiting for me on the platform; it was a very intense encounter. Both of us had prison behind us, and none of the friends we had been together with two years ago were free. I stayed in Frankfurt for a few days, and we talked about ourselves, our feelings, our plans. … He was rediscovering the feeling of being free again but was clear about the fact that he wanted to get back to the guerrilla as soon as possible. He also said that those in prison had to be freed; they were committed, and he wanted to continue the struggle with them.

Some time after that, I met up again with the comrade from the RAF. Once again, I had carefully prepared my journey with the help of my city map, as well as other maps and timetables. This time, a friend of Kay's took me part way by motorbike, so that I could shake off those constantly tailing me.

I talked about my travels, about Helmut, and about the people I had met. The comrade was more open this time and more relaxed. He told me that the RAF was now a small group for whom life had become very difficult following the arrests in 1972. They lacked the political and practical experience that the founding members had had, and the left had become afraid of having anything to do with the RAF. He asked if I also thought that the prisoners had to be freed. For the new members, it was clear that without Andreas, Gudrun, Ulrike, Holger, and Jan they would never be able to develop the strength they needed for the struggle in West Germany. He told me Andreas had warned them to be careful in their dealings with me at first. Despite this, they still wanted to know if I wanted to help them. It wasn't about my becoming a member of the RAF or a guerrilla fighter; they wanted to know if I would help build the infrastructure that those in prison would need to get around after being freed. I agreed to do this.

I rarely saw Helmut anymore, assuming he had also met with the comrades from the RAF and was preparing to go underground. I found out later that this was, indeed, the case.

I met the comrade from the RAF for a third and a fourth time. "The action to free the prisoners will be underway soon," he said. "We assume that afterward many people will be arrested as a preventive measure or out of revenge. You will almost certainly be among them. In any case, none of those known to the pigs will be able to move about freely for a while. We need to get a hold of apartments, and everybody at risk will have to go underground before things start. Do you want to?"

I had no idea what kind of action they were planning, and I didn't feel as if I had the right to ask. That was the business of those living underground, and I wasn't meant to be part of that—nor did I want to be. For reasons of safety and principle ("each of us should only know about what they themselves are directly involved in"), I wasn't to be informed about it. However, I did want the prisoners out of prison.

I had never thought I would have to decide whether or not to "go underground" so quickly. I had wanted to take more time for myself, to gain more political experience, to make some progress, and now I was supposed to suddenly make a move. But why not? In the three and a half months since I had been released, I hadn't found a group I wanted to join. Everywhere I went, it was different than I had imagined it to be while in prison. I saw my choice as being either to support the other prisoners after they had been freed or to not do so and risk being sent back to prison myself.

Reorganization of the RAF

In early June 1973, I returned to life underground. It was four months since my release from prison.

I managed to shake off the "silent companions" who were constantly at my heels by working out an exact plan of the public transport I would use, and when and where I could transfer without any waiting time. Although it was pretty easy to get rid of them, I checked for several hours afterward to make sure that my followers were gone for good. Then I took the train to West Berlin and went to a "conspiratorial apartment": these were safehouses, apartments maintained under false names by members or supporters of various left-wing groups in West Germany for the purposes of housing people who were living underground or who were on the run. A woman was waiting there who was going to help me. She cut and bleached my hair, then took a photo of me and inserted it in a fake passport that had been prepared for me. This was always somewhat tricky because of my height.

With my new documents in my possession, I headed for Rotterdam, Holland, where I met up with Helmut Pohl and two others. They told me they had worked out a plan with some people from Al-Fatah in Lebanon to get the prisoners free by hijacking a plane, and that they were waiting for news from the Palestinians. The plan was for a group under Palestinian command but including members of the RAF to hijack an Israeli plane in Amsterdam.

At the time, it was clear to some within the Palestinian groups that they needed the support of the radical left in Europe, because the critical material support that made Israel's existence possible came from Europe and the

US. Since the 1960s, the Middle East, with all its oil wells, had become increasingly important to the West. For us, Israel was first and foremost the imperialist bastion of the oil-dependent industrial nations. Ulrike once told us that before 1967 she had actively supported Israel, the kibbutz movement in particular. The memory of Auschwitz meant that she too demanded material support for Israel, something that the West German governments after 1945 only paid grudgingly and slowly. During the 1967 Six-Day War, however, the Springer press ridiculed the fleeing Arabs with insulting racism, praising the efficiency of the Israeli Army, and many on the left changed their position on Israel. The fate of the Palestinian people became critical when, following their expulsion by Israel, they were forced to live in huge camps, without a future, without a country, serving merely as pawns in the strategic designs of others, including the Arab states. In 1970, Palestinian guerrilla groups decided to hijack planes to draw attention to their plight and to push the international community to put pressure on Israel. The hijackings achieved their objectives, and, as of 1973, nobody had been hurt. We considered these to be legitimate attacks against a state that was trampling on the fundamental rights of another people.

It wasn't until later that we realized that this is not an acceptable form of action for revolutionaries, because the lives of many people who have nothing to do with the struggle are automatically put at risk. It took many years, however, for us to come to this conclusion.

When I arrived in Rotterdam, the operation had already been planned and preparations made. Several Palestinians had come to Amsterdam to nail down the last details, and they had brought weapons with them, mainly machine guns. The Israeli plane that was scheduled to land and take off from Amsterdam was to be seized by a mixed group consisting of two Palestinians and two Germans. We were just waiting for the go-ahead signal.

For weeks, we waited. When nothing happened and we got sick of waiting, one of our representatives flew to Lebanon to meet with Ali Hassan Salameh (who we knew as Abu Hassan), the Palestinian in charge. He let us know that the situation in the Middle East was coming to a head on all levels, and as a result no joint operations could be carried out at the present time. Abu Hassan was Yasser Arafat's security chief and represented the radical wing of Al-Fatah, which was in favor of working with the RAF. Arafat himself was always opposed to such cooperation. In 1973, Israel stepped up its attacks on Lebanon, where Al-Fatah had its main base in the refugee camps. This caused intense conflict among the Palestinians about how to proceed. We didn't understand Abu Hassan's reply. There had already been several delays in preparing the operation. We thought that the Palestinians perhaps didn't want to carry out joint operations with us but didn't want to say so directly. It was not until October, when the fourth war in the Middle East broke out, the Yom Kippur War, that we understood what Abu Hassan had meant when he had told us that things were heating up on all fronts.

Years later, when I was back in prison, I read in the newspaper that this Palestinian friend, who had been important to us, had been killed by a Mossad commando unit.

All of our plans and thinking had been focused on this hijacking; when any hope of carrying out the operation disappeared beyond the horizon, we had to consider other options. What could we do now? Again and again it became clear to us that we needed more members. We went over the people we knew who we thought might want to work with the RAF. One of us travelled to Hamburg, contacted some comrades and organized an apartment, and then the others followed. I was the most well-known of those being hunted for in West Germany and, therefore, the one most in danger. For this reason, but also because the others had had far more discussions and had been more involved in planning the hijacking and were far more determined to engage in armed politics as the RAF, I initially stayed behind, alone in the Rotterdam flat. Perhaps the expected signal would still come from Lebanon.

The uncertainty and the waiting were very difficult for me. I had burned all my bridges, so what was I to do now? I had gone back underground to lay the groundwork for freeing the imprisoned comrades, to make new contacts, to find apartments, and to forge papers. It seemed that these activities had come to a dead end, and if I really wanted the comrades to be freed I would have to create the conditions for that to happen and plan and carry out the operation myself. This idea didn't appeal to me, but I could see no other way.

After about two or three weeks, someone showed up at the apartment to tell me that I was to return to West Germany, that they had a new place. I took the weapon I had had for some time, but which I had never carried with me when walking around Rotterdam, hid it under a scarf in my handbag, and went by train to Hamburg. There, I learned that closer contact had been established with Christa Eckes, whom I had met during my trial when she was working as a legal assistant for my lawyer. After spending a long time with the Trotskyists and sick of all the fights about theory, she had left them and was looking for an opportunity to put her politics into practice. Having followed my trial, she had become interested in the RAF and the prisoners.

There had also been ongoing discussions with Kay while I had been away, and both Christa and Kay wanted to join the group. Christa had also brought along Wolfgang Beer, whom she had known for quite some time. He had also been active with the Trotskyists, leaving them at the same time as Christa. The intense confrontation around the house on Eckhofstraße had been the final straw that had pushed them both to come to the RAF.

We were a disorganized group and the most unlikely candidates for being able to actually accomplish anything. None of us had the political experience or know-how necessary to organize clandestine work. We hardly knew each other and had no experience working together. What united us and pushed us forward was our shared desire to free the prisoners. We had no doubt whatsoever that we would be unable to achieve very much without the founding members of the RAF, and that their involvement would be critical for the continued existence of the urban guerrilla strategy. We knew that it would take years for us to acquire the political experience and knowledge that Andreas, Gudrun, Ulrike, Holger, and Jan possessed. And whether we would ever be able to develop the imagination, initiative, and drive they had was doubtful.

We were lacking in everything, and we had hardly any political or material support. We had no infrastructure, no logistics, no apartments, hardly any weapons, and no money, and there were problems with ID documents and passports. We tried to tackle everything at once. Two or three of us in Hamburg, two or three in Frankfurt, two or three on the move. We were stealing cars, forging papers, casing banks, trying to establish political contacts, organizing weapons, reading political statements and papers, carrying out discussions about our mistakes and our plans.

We got ourselves into a real tangle with all of this. We applied ourselves and tapped every possible resource in an attempt to make our ideas reality, to put things into practice and do more than just talk. However, it was just too much—the pressure from the state, which was hunting for us with everything at its disposal, the pressure from the left, which wanted us to stop, and the internal pressure we exerted on ourselves.

We didn't take any time to get to know each other or to gain more practical experience together. We split up immediately. As I was well-known in Hamburg, I went to Frankfurt with Kay to try to get an apartment, money, and weapons and to establish contact with people who might support us. Helmut, who came from Frankfurt and, therefore, felt he might be recognized there, stayed in Hamburg with Ilse Stachowiak, who was left over from the RAF group that had been arrested in 1972. Christa, who was not on the wanted list, and who had the most contacts in Hamburg, also stayed there. Another person from our group had been arrested during one of his many border crossings before we even got underway. After Wolfgang joined the group, he also stayed in Hamburg for a while; he was from the city and knew his way around.

Kay and I started looking around in Frankfurt. Helmut and Ilse visited us often, and sometimes we went to Hamburg.

We visited people I had met during my travels after I got out of prison. We also visited some people with whom we had lost contact following the 1972 arrests; we were directed to these people by secret messages sent by the prisoners. This was how, one day, we came to be standing in front of "Pfirsich's" workshop. "Pfirsich" was Dirk Hoff's nickname. He was pleased when we told him who we were. "Man, how fucked up was that when they were all arrested! At first, I thought they'd get me too, and after having heard nothing from you lot for so long, I thought you didn't exist anymore. What are you planning now? What do you need?"

He called his girlfriend, a North American, small, with short blonde hair, and very likeable, so that we could meet her too. "She's great, we do everything together." The first thing he did was weld some "corkscrews" for us so that we could steal cars. Then he helped us repair and modify our weapons, which he was a master at. All the while, he wanted to talk to us about our past mistakes and our prospects for the future. Later on, after I had been arrested, I read his statements in the press and couldn't believe it. He insisted he had been forced at gunpoint by Holger Meins to cooperate with them, and he reinforced all of the clichés that were being used as part of the psychological war: Andreas, the stupid, big-mouthed gang boss who did everything wrong; Holger, the ice-cold killer.

Nobody asked why he had continued to work with us after those who had allegedly forced him to had already been in prison for more than a year.

We met friends who had often worked with Ulrike and the other prisoners, and who had assumed that everything was over after all the arrests. They were suspicious when we turned up, thinking the police were on to them and were trying to set a trap. Once we got to talking, they realized they could trust us and helped us find apartments and make contact with other supporters. Of the various matters we discussed, the stories about the founding phase of the RAF were of particular interest to Kay and me.

One day, I travelled to Karlsruhe to look for the people I had met during the solidarity hunger strike in front of the Federal Court of Justice in February. I couldn't remember their full names or their exact addresses, only the area they lived in. I walked around the town for hours hoping to find their apartments or perhaps bump into them. At some point, I met someone who told me they had moved away. Long after my second arrest, they joined the RAF.

We also met with a group that was organizing solidarity for the IRA. The liberation movements in Ireland and in the Basque country had flared up again in the 1960s and were engaging in guerrilla struggle. With the comrades there, we talked about the political contradictions within the IRA and asked if they were interested in cooperating with us. They were not against the armed struggle, but they were not in favor of the RAF either.

We went to intellectuals and writers, to Heinrich Böll's son and to his Indian wife and to Karin Struck. We didn't know them personally, but from their statements we saw that they sympathized with us. We wanted to get to know them and see if they would work with us. They were friendly but rejected any kind of cooperation.

When Helmut and Ilse came to Frankfurt, we didn't get on very well. They thought that Kay and I worked badly, that we weren't getting anything done, and that we didn't have the right attitude when dealing with people. Kay and I thought they weren't doing any better than we were. We distanced ourselves from one another and became competitive. We felt at a disadvantage, because there were only two of us, and we had to work in a city that was largely unknown to us, while the Hamburg group had four members, two of whom were very familiar with the city.

Through various channels, we had discussions with Andreas and the other prisoners. We lacked technical know-how and asked their advice, for example, about forging passports and stealing cars. We sought guidance from those in prison about our plans to free them; but what they suggested was impossible, way beyond our capabilities.

We discussed again and again how we could free those in prison. Perhaps we could kidnap somebody important? But who? A businessperson or a politician? A German or an American? We never got beyond such questions.

After we had been forced to give up on our plan with the Palestinians and the hijacking, Andreas worked out a detailed plan for us to free him that required a completely different structure and other logistics, which we just weren't able to set up. We should have destroyed his plan, as we would never have been able to implement it, not then or later—but we kept it, like so many other things. When we were arrested in February 1974, the plan was found by the police and the Federal Prosecutor's Office made the most of it, using it to prove there had always been plans to free the prisoners. It was used to justify the continuation of the inhumane conditions at Stammheim prison. With this mistake, we had given State Security exactly what they had been looking for. Andreas was very critical of us, because we didn't come up with any ideas, any plans, or any actions. He was right. But we had tried and couldn't change matters, and neither could he.

Eventually, Andreas convinced his lawyer Eberhard Becker to join us. Eberhard was dissatisfied with his work, and both of them were of the opinion that he would make all the difference in improving our situation and our prospects. Of course, that wasn't the case. Rather, we now had a new guy in the "group" who we hardly knew, and, what's more, he was full of Andreas's ideas about the direction we should take, which didn't bear any real relationship to our group process or to what we had been thinking of. The competitive fights and conflicts among us got worse and almost led to our complete collapse.

To solve our money problems, we decided to rob a bank. As far as we were concerned, that was a legitimate way to get money that had been stolen from the people for our cause. Ulrike had once written: "Some people say robbing banks is not political. Since when is the question of financing a political organization not a political question? The urban guerrilla in Latin America calls bank robberies 'expropriation actions.' Nobody is claiming that robbing banks will be all it takes to change the oppressive social order. For revolutionary organizations, it mainly represents the solution to their financial problems. It makes logical sense, because there is no other solution to the financial problem. It makes political sense, because it is an expropriation action. It makes tactical sense, because it is a proletarian action. It makes strategic sense, because it finances the guerilla."

First, we had to find a suitable bank and steal the getaway cars. We stole cars the way I had learned before going to prison, but we also tried other approaches. For example, we observed the owner of a big white Mercedes over a long period of time, and saw that at the same time every day on his way home from work, he would drive along a stretch of road that wasn't clearly visible. One day, we overtook him, waved him down pretending to want something from him, asking him to get out of the car to help us. Then we jumped in his car and drove away. One of us followed in a second car, listening to the police radio, just to make sure. We had rented a garage beforehand, and we parked the Mercedes there, so that we could change its appearance without being interrupted.

More than twenty-five years later, I can no longer remember the details of the bank robbery. I had buried them deep at the back of my mind so that I would not be able to put anyone at risk. Now, even though there is no risk of endangering anyone, the memories are simply beyond my recall.

The only thing I see before me is the following scene: we all run out of the bank and jump into the Volkswagen van that is waiting for us with its motor running. The driver revs the engine and rounds the next corner so fast that for a moment the van is balancing on two wheels, and we almost tip over. While we are all changing into the clothes we had prepared beforehand, I notice a deep cut on Christa's thigh. She is completely calm and, in the blink of an eye, she tears off a strip of cloth from somewhere, ties it tightly around her leg, and then continues to change into new clothes like the rest of us, as if nothing had happened. (Because of this, Christa would be the only one of us ever convicted for the bank robbery, the injury being used as circumstantial evidence.) After changing clothes, we go our separate ways, and I get on a bus with one other person from our group. We are carrying the money from the robbery in a plastic bag, as if we had just come from the supermarket.

In Frankfurt, we met several times with Wilfried "Bony" Böse and Brigitte Kuhlmann. They were in the middle of organizing their own clandestine structure and setting up the Revolutionary Cells (Revolutionäre Zellen, RZ). They had different political and organizational ideas than the RAF. They thought it was important that all members of the RZ stay aboveground for as long as possible, remaining in their usual circumstances and continuing to go to work. Just from the way they dressed, you could tell that they were in a different kind of left. We thought that whole scene was unrealistic and lacked seriousness. We thought they were only playing with the idea of revolution, without any real interest in actually doing anything practical about it. We were convinced that their strategy provided the Federal Office for the Protection of the Constitution (Bundesamt für Verfassungsschutz, BfV) with too many opportunities to infiltrate them.

We discussed carrying out coordinated actions with the RZ following the military putsch in Chile, in September 1973. We from the RAF wanted to attack covert weapons transports that were on their way to Chile via the Hamburg and Bremerhaven ports. We eventually had to abandon these plans, as any such operation would have required all our energy and would have brought us even further from our goal of freeing the prisoners. It was in November 1973 that the RZ carried out its first operation, attacking American ITT subsidiaries in West Germany because of their support for the coup against the Chilean government. Brigitte and "Bony" also helped us obtain weapons.

Almost three years later, both of them would die in Entebbe when an Israeli military strike force attacked an Air France plane that had been hijacked by a Palestinian commando unit that "Bony" and Brigitte were part of. The hijackers demanded the release of fifty-three prisoners held in different countries, including six in West Germany. All of the members of the guerrilla unit died at Entebbe airport. Afterward, when the newspapers reported that the passengers had been separated into Jews and non-Jews, I couldn't believe it. It seemed like a typical media lie to me. It wasn't until later that I began to think more about the difficult tightrope walk that separated anti-Zionism from antisemitism.

We did not have any contact with the 2nd of June Movement, a conglomerate of various militant groups in West Berlin that had joined forces in early 1972. We never travelled to West Berlin ourselves, but we knew that there had been fierce arguments between Andreas and Gudrun and the members of the 2JM about the criteria for political operations, ending with the two groups going their separate ways. The RAF described the 2JM as populist, saying that they "only looked for people's applause." The RAF wanted to carry out strategic operations that hit at the centers of power, in particular against the US, which treated West Germany "like a colony."

Two of us traveled to Italy to meet with comrades from the Red Brigades. I traveled with someone else to France to speak with members of a Portuguese armed organization that had asked to meet with us; they needed some help falsifying documents. We communicated in French, which I could speak quite well. Still, it was difficult to understand one another, the French that the two comrades from Portugal spoke sounded pretty Portuguese, and their formulations were also strange to us. Their language consisted of a mixture of Maoist-Marxist vocabulary that we seemed to use differently. And what they told us was even more unfamiliar to us: they mainly organized within the Portuguese colonial army. Both comrades had already participated in Portugal's wars in Africa, even though they were still young, about the same age as us, barely twenty. They said that that was where the force to overthrow the Salazar regime could be found. They were coordinating with African liberation movements in Angola, Mozambique, and Guinea-Bissau.

"We mainly carry out acts of sabotage. Many of the comrades from our organization have been tortured and killed. But the fight isn't going to last much longer, the fascist colonial regime is about to fall." Carrying out political work within an army was something we couldn't even begin to imagine. Armies were always part of the other side. US soldiers had been helped by members of the German left to desert during the Vietnam War, but what we were now hearing from these Portuguese sounded like something out of this world.

We had met on the street and went for a walk in a park, the two of them nervously looking around us at all times. I handed over the documents on forgery after explaining our basic techniques. Translating everything wasn't a problem; they said they had already arranged for that. "Do you need weapons?" they asked. One of their most important tasks, they told us, was to provide the African liberation movements with weapons they stole from the Portuguese army stocks. They could get something for us if we wanted. We arranged to meet again some weeks later, but nothing came of that meeting.

In autumn 1973, some guy in Hamburg who had rented an apartment for us snitched. The Hamburg BfV decided not to arrest the first person who entered the apartment but to carry out long-term surveillance to identify everyone living underground, and then capture us all together in one big operation. The noose was constantly tightening.

One time, Kay and I were riding around Cologne in a car; I was driving. All of a sudden, I noticed a car behind us in the rear mirror. The two guys I saw in it made my blood run cold—I knew they were pigs. We began to systematically check whether cars drove past us repeatedly or stayed close to us. It didn't take us long to realize that we were being watched by a large contingent of cars. We considered how we could get away. We hadn't been to Cologne that often and didn't know our way around, and the only thing we could think of was to drive to the underground garage at the Cathedral.

First, we tried to lure the observation cars to another area of the city. Then we drove as fast as we could straight to the underground garage, parked the car on the middle parking level and ran to the stairway that led right up to Cathedral Square. While running, we pulled off our coats and I tied a scarf around my hair. As we were rushing across the road, we saw the observation cars sealing off the car park. None of them paid us any attention, because they assumed we were still in the parking garage.

Even after we were arrested, we could not make sense of this attempt to capture us. We later discovered from our case files that it had been a competitive attempt by the Federal BfV to win the glory of making a successful "terrorist arrest." This despite the fact that their attempt clashed with the aforementioned plan of the Hamburg BfV, which was waiting to arrest us all in one fell swoop after an extended period of observation.

The bank robbery had been successful, but, apart from that, little of what we attempted worked out properly, and we had zero success pursuing our actual goal of freeing Andreas, Ulrike, and the others. Instead, we began to argue, and the more they had us under surveillance, the more we began to mistrust each other—all the while failing to draw any conclusions from our failings. We didn't give the people who wanted to work with us a chance. We weren't able to turn useful contacts into sustainable relationships. It was awful.

At that time, and also later, I treated others self-righteously, arrogantly, and with contempt. In my conviction that I had taken the only possible and correct path, I measured everything and everybody by my own yardstick. One woman who I had long been in contact with worked in an important American military institution. She looked around and found opportunities for us to carry out a bomb attack on the computer center and asked to play an active role in the attack. I reacted to her request with a point-blank refusal. I dismissed her willingness as a complete overestimation of her own capabilities, criticized her into the ground, and then, on my say-so, we broke off all contact with her.

During the winter months, all of us had noticed agents carrying out surveillance, but, at first, we didn't think it had anything to do with us. We simply couldn't imagine and didn't want to admit that the police could have picked up our trail. Later on, when encounters with the surveillance teams and attempts to arrest us became more frequent, we began to have an extremely subjective view of the situation, which was often far removed from objective reality. As we saw it, anybody who saw policemen was looking for a way out of the struggle, and anybody who felt they were under surveillance had problems with clandestinity. We were hoisted by our own petard, dismissing reality as a projection created by our own minds.

On the night of February 4, 1974, four of us (Wolfgang and Eberhard were also in Frankfurt) were spending the night in a safehouse on the top floor of a new apartment block. Suddenly, we were woken by noise and bright lights. The apartment was surrounded by a huge number of police, and the entire building was lit up by very bright floodlights. We could hear a helicopter above and a voice on a loudspeaker ordering us to surrender and come out of the apartment, unarmed, naked, and with our hands in the air. The door to the flat burst open with a loud bang, and through the windows we could see heavily armed police on the roof.

At exactly the same time, Christa, Ilse, and Helmut were being arrested in Hamburg. Because of the date of our arrest, we were referred to as the "4.2 Group" from that point on. The perfect ending to the previous six shitty months.

All four of us stepped into the apartment entryway, naked, with our hands up. The entire stairwell was overflowing with heavily armed police in protective gear. I was the only woman, I had to stand halfway down the stairs naked, surrounded by young policemen. After the initial tension eased, the pigs began to make comments about my body. It was about half an hour before the officer in charge wrapped a coat around me. I felt absolutely degraded and humiliated.

In the Dead Wing

The next day, my Frankfurt lawyer Armin Golzem came to see me at Preungesheim prison. I felt exhausted with life, utterly worn out, unable to think straight. Even walking was difficult. Golzem, entirely derisive about our defeat, had brought the newspapers with him. Our arrest was the top story, of course, and once again my face and name were on the front pages, along with those of Helmut Pohl and Ilse Stachowiak. I learned that on the night of our arrest hourly radio broadcasts had claimed that the RAF was threatening to use SAM-7 missiles to attack the World Cup at Hamburg's sports stadium on June 22, unless all political prisoners were granted amnesty on May 1.

In the thoroughly depressed state that I was in, I was incapable of reacting, but the whole situation reminded me of when they were preparing to arrest Holger, Jan-Carl, and Andreas. Who was to blame? This time it was clear beyond a doubt that State Security had planned and prepared our arrests over a long period of time. I could hear the other prisoners, and when I was taken to the showers or to my lawyer, I could see some of them, but all contact was strictly forbidden, and we didn't even try. I repeatedly found myself ruminating about the past year; my overwhelming feeling was shame at my own incompetence.

After four weeks in Preungesheim prison in Frankfurt, I was flown by helicopter to Lübeck and brought to the wing that contained the women's prison medical unit. This was a flat-roofed building completely cut off from the rest of the prison, with its own walled-in yard outside of the rest of the grounds. When I arrived there, all of the medical cells were occupied.

In the days that followed, the guards removed prisoners from the wing every day; when they were finished, only one other prisoner apart from me remained. She was in a cell at the other end of the building, a sick woman resigned to her fate, who didn't respond to any of my attempts to make contact with her. I had carefully noted the transfers of the other prisoners, thinking that if this woman was also transferred, then I would find myself in a Dead Wing. What I didn't want to admit to myself was that I was already in a Dead Wing. Even when, in the following months, one or two prisoners were transferred to the sick bay for a short time, it didn't change my situation one bit, because I heard nothing from them.

During my period underground, toward the end of 1973, I read Ulrike's reports from the Dead Wing, which was located in the medical wing at Cologne's Ossendorf prison. Her situation had sparked a broad movement against this form of torture. The Dead Wing is the core element of a cleverly devised scientific form of torture that remains invisible, both in its use and in its immediate impact. So-called white torture doesn't depend on physical violence. It doesn't use punches or electric shocks. Instead, it uses absolute human isolation, depriving the person subjected to it of every form of live communication. Even with a radio, books, and maybe a television, the very substance of a person's soul dies, while their outer shell remains unscathed.

The reports by Ulrike from the Dead Wing had shaken me to the core. Despite its cruelty, the use of this specific form of torture seemed logical to me; the enemy fights its toughest opponent with its fiercest weapon. Ulrike occupied a position of central importance for the guerrilla movement and was, therefore, clearly identified as an enemy of the state. She was one of the movement's founders, and she had become one of its living symbols.

But why were the methods of the Dead Wing being applied to me? It's true that I had become a public figure thanks to the media, but I judged myself above all by what I had planned and by what I had either failed to achieve or had done wrong. I was desperately looking for a reason why this torture was being used against me but could find none. Was I really such a big threat?

I felt like a failure. As reason remained beyond my grasp, I fantasized that I wasn't really in a Dead Wing. My world was turned upside down, and I was no longer able to tell the difference between what went on inside my head and external reality. When the last prisoner in the wing was finally transferred from her cell, I broke down completely.

At the time, I didn't realize that the measures used against presumed or actual revolutionaries are never directed solely against the individual. Such measures also serve to deter others, so that the idea of revolution is strangled and a feeling of powerlessness spreads.

The Dead Wing was a reaction to the public image of some kind of "highly dangerous terrorist" that was being propagated by the media. In the press, I was labelled the "leader of the 4.2 Group," and now the state apparatus was using one of its most vicious instruments to destroy me, the alleged head of the revolution. As I wasn't aware that this was their goal, I was unable to defend myself. The Dead Wing had done its job.

The first time I was in prison, I was in solitary confinement, isolated from the other prisoners, but I could see them when they were exercising in the yard, and they could see me. I heard them twenty-four hours a day, because they lived in the same building as I did, even if the cells beside, above, and below mine had been vacated. I heard them laughing, calling to one another, arguing, and crying. And, time and again, other prisoners tried to contact me, despite it being forbidden; they talked to me from window to window or tried to slip notes undetected under my door. I was alone and shut out, but I was in a building that was alive.

The Dead Wing represents a whole other level of solitary confinement. I was alone with nothing around me but a great emptiness. Alone in a completely isolated building. I saw and heard nothing from the rest of the prison where the other prisoners were housed. There was nothing but endless silence. No sound, no back and forth, no laughing, no crying. Only me. In this kind of emptiness, contours disappear. Your sense of your own body disappears, even your sense of your own existence. And the walls, the iron bed frame, what few objects are in your cell, even your very movements, all merge to become one undefinable sameness.

I was in a really bad state. I cried every morning when I woke up, not knowing how I was going to make it through the day. I was aware every single day that I was battling insanity. I made friends with the spiders and began to study these creatures, the only other living beings in the cell. I learned to tell them apart by their colors, shapes, and sizes, another exercise designed to stop myself from going crazy. The effort this required helped me close the hole where otherwise madness would have seeped in. For hours on end, I observed the sparrows and the blackbirds in the yard, just to catch sight of something living. When the small sparrows stole food from the larger blackbirds, it was one of my few moments of joy. It took an enormous effort for me to read, and writing was almost impossible. By 7:00 p.m., I was so exhausted that I fell into a deep, leaden sleep that would last until the following morning.

The only people I saw or heard were the female guards, when they brought food or came to take me out to the yard for my exercise period. In my hunger for human contact, I had to constantly struggle against seeking a friendly gesture from them. One day they would be friendly, the next day hostile, and this unsettled me. It took some time before I realized I would have to distance myself from them to avoid becoming their pawn, which was obviously their objective. The same female guard came all the time, accompanied by the deputy prison director and a male guard. The two women looked like peasants—strong, broad in stature, with red cheeks, their cold, keen eyes keeping a close watch on me at all times.

Prison Director Greif was a skinny little man whom I rarely saw, although I did feel the effects of his sanctions. It was still damned cold in late February and early March 1974. A cold cell is one of the main problems every prisoner has to deal with. You never get warm. I was given prison overalls and a thin, short cardigan. No prison coat and no warm jacket for me. Greif refused permission for me to have my own coat "for security reasons."

He and his deputy director ordered the other prisoners to stand with their faces to the wall whenever I passed one of them on my way to have my weekly shower. It was as if I had the evil eye or an illness that was so contagious it could be contracted by merely looking at me. One time, we passed a prisoner who was cleaning the floor, and she looked up, but the moment she saw it was me she stiffened and turned her face to the wall. I got a hard lump in my throat and felt like I was choking.

Every fourteen days was "shopping" day, when the prisoners could buy some extra food from a guy who came from outside the prison. I wasn't allowed to go myself, of course, but had to give my shopping list to the director, who then brought me some of the things I had ordered the following day. I always waited for him to arrive with burning hunger and stuffed my face with the fruit, biscuits, and cheese as soon as they were delivered. Every time, hardly an hour would pass before I had devoured everything, leaving me with an aching belly, a heavy head, and legs that felt like they weighed a ton. That didn't matter; at least it interrupted the monotony and emptiness of the days. I could feel myself again, even if it hurt, as I had to strain to digest everything, and that awakened my ability to think.

I assumed the reason I felt so bad was because I had screwed up so completely in my one year of freedom. It never occurred to me then that my wretched state was due to the harsh prison conditions. I spent the whole time looking inward, rummaging about my inner self, and then doing it all over again, instead of seeing the external reality.

Since my first arrest in 1971, the prison conditions had changed completely for all RAF prisoners. Many people who wanted to visit us were refused by the courts, because they were seen as "sympathizers." Many left-wing newspapers, pamphlets, and written statements were confiscated, because they "endorsed criminal activities." This argument was applied to any form of resistance, no matter where— whether in Chile against the fascist military, in South Africa against racist violence, in Iran against the terror of the Shah's regime, or the Palestinians' struggle for their right to live and against their expulsion and occupation by Israel. The courts censored all information of this kind, because they thought reading about the struggles of other liberation movements might encourage us in our own political convictions.

To give just one example, a ruling by my Hamburg custodial judge read as follows:

1. The written works and newspapers listed below are not to be delivered to prisoners and are to be placed with the prisoners' possessions in storage.

Informationsdienst no. 37, 38, and no. 40
Chile News no. 16
MIR, Chile Documentation 1
Informationsdienst no. 42
Documents from the Chile Committee

The listed broadcasts are not to be delivered …

All of the written works on this list condone armed struggle against the existing order, believe it to be right and necessary, and see it as a way to achieve the goal of changing existing conditions.

These written works are a threat to order in the prison institution. This also applies for prisoners in solitary confinement, because it is not possible to fully prevent such writings from being spread from prisoner to prisoner by passing them through windows, for example. In this way, prisoners might be encouraged and incited to insubordination.

This measure does not constitute an infringement on freedom of expression or opinion. As the listed writings call for breaches of the law to be carried out, at least indirectly, they are no longer covered by the Basic Law (Art. 5 ii Basic Law).

Isbarn
Local Court Judge

Cells were often searched and the guards tore everything apart, leaving nothing unturned; our defense documents were examined, and every kind of personal record was confiscated. There wasn't anything they couldn't get their hands on, not even the fragments of thought I put down on paper in an attempt to bring some semblance of order to the chaos in my head.

Hunger Strike and Death

Prisoners from the RAF and its political milieu were scattered across many different prisons throughout West Germany. To counter this separation and the effects of solitary confinement, the prisoners created *Info* in 1973. This was a form of written correspondence passed back and forth between the prisoners via the resistance post. We used *Info* to discuss trial strategies, political analysis, and, above all, to write about ourselves and our situations in prison. *Info* became a symbol of how we could organize in prison and still continue to fight for every single one of us, to prevent solitary confinement from separating and crushing us.

These letters contained political discussions between the RAF founding members that I found fascinating. They discussed the long-term goals and methods of revolution. Their aim was not to establish a new revolutionary party that would address the question of power only to assume power itself. If the movement were institutionalized, they believed, this could only lead to the kind of rigidity that was exemplified by the GDR or the Soviet Union. Even if the RAF repeatedly expressed its solidarity with these countries, it never shared their political ideas. It was impossible to come up with a precise model for a new and just future society, they argued, because the road to get there was so long, and it was the experiences that were had during the struggle itself that would give rise to new possibilities and ideas. The primary goal was to bring about the collapse of imperialism by the Third World liberation movements under the protection of the socialist states, working together with the resistance movements within the metropoles of the US and Europe, and to paralyze this First World to such an extent that it was no longer capable of functioning. Not until after the downfall of imperialism would an opportunity for the real liberation of all humanity present itself. Revolution limited to one country was something that the RAF considered impossible, because the unequal balance of power would always lead to the wheel of history being turned backward.

To provide a foundation for their thinking, they studied the revolutionary classics by Lenin, Rosa Luxemburg, Lukács, and Bakunin and tried to analyze the experiences of the liberation movements in the Third World over the previous twenty years, discussing the work of recent theoreticians like Régis Debray, for example.

In April 1974, the Portuguese colonial regime collapsed. After a long period of violence, the Carnation Revolution, as it was called, had occurred without bloodshed. I remembered the two comrades we had met in France, and I now understood what they had been telling us. Young soldiers who had waged war in Africa refused to continue this war, which had taken the lives of so many Portuguese soldiers. The streets of Portugal became places of celebration where the people danced, cheering for Major Otelo and the other young officers with carnations in their hands. Every day, the newspapers I received in my cell brought reports about the developments in Portugal.

Hopefully the Yankees wouldn't intervene like they had done the previous year in Chile, helping Augusto Pinochet to victory over President Allende, who had been elected by the people. I decided that my "area of work" in the coming years in prison was going to be the Portuguese colonies in Africa, which were obviously going to become independent sometime soon. I wanted to know more about them and ordered reading materials from my lawyer, from bookshops, and from the comrades who wrote to me. I asked them to send me whatever they could get their hands on.

However, the longer I was isolated in the Dead Wing, the less able I was to concentrate and to imagine life outside of my cell. The world began to shrink to only myself and my fight for survival within those four walls. A rift opened up separating me from the other RAF prisoners. I felt shut out and lost my ability to relate to others, becoming obsessed with myself.

When I received mail, the discussions about developments among the Tupamaros in Uruguay or Willy Brandt's resignation no longer interested me. Instead, I looked through the letters with trembling hands, to see if they contained some criticism of me. If I didn't find anything, I would sit back down in my chair, relieved. Whenever I found a snippet somewhere that was critical of me, my heart would start pounding violently. For hours afterward, I would be unable to read anything at all and would think of nothing but those few words against me.

I was completely overreacting, of course, but a harsh tone did predominate in *Info*. Criticism was often used as a cudgel, and it could become a form of self-flagellation. The language used was often unbearable, and relations between us were not comradely. This clearly reflected the brutality of the situation we found ourselves in.

I no longer remember who wrote this sentence in a letter dated July 1974: "It is not the aim of these questions to set up an Inquisition." From Jan, maybe, or from Gudrun. However, the longer it went on, the more this process of criticism and self-criticism was moving toward exactly that. The words we used to attack each other and to castigate ourselves exemplified this tendency: treachery, collaboration, pig, bastard— words with which we described our own thoughts and feelings, anything that didn't seem to fit in with our ideas of morality and proper conduct. Using the word "treachery" instead of "mistake" called the person themself into question, fully condemning his or her motives and efforts. When

I read these letters today, almost twenty-five years later, my impression is that, in *Info*, the torture forced its own language upon us—just as it did within the small groups of political prisoners in the cell blocks—and we reacted by taking it out on one another.

We wanted to give everything to the struggle, but we also rubbed salt in each other's wounds, causing further agony. We wanted to make ourselves fully "a function of the struggle," and we felt right in what we were doing and duty-bound to control and analyze each other in everything we said and did. We wanted a collective process, but the differences that existed in experience, knowledge, initiative, and courage also created positions of power.

It was Andreas who made the major decisions and who remained untouchable. One story making the rounds was that during one of the first minor hunger strikes, someone found out he had eaten some chicken—something that nobody else in the group could have done without being subjected to a barrage of scathing criticism labelling them a "traitor to the hunger strike and the collective." Andreas was constantly searching for practical things to do, even in prison, in solitary confinement. And he was able to study in a disciplined manner even under those harsh conditions, gaining a vast amount of knowledge on a variety of subjects, while also paying attention to everyone in the group. But nobody criticized him and, with that gesture of his—"Come on, surely you must understand that!"—or his quick judgements, he could hurt people a great deal, or even silence them.

Completely alone in the separate medical wing of Lübeck prison, I lost myself and began to live within projections of my own mind, becoming very afraid of people. It was a vicious circle. On the one hand, I had a tremendous hunger for company and to be close to people, but, on the other hand, there was this tremendous fear of others. Such is the madness that solitary confinement was striving to achieve.

The perverseness of this method of torture is that it intends to render "its object" unable to communicate by stripping away living communication. That is exactly what happened to me.

Holger somehow realized what was going on and wrote me a letter asking what was wrong with me. He tried to help, by reminding me of the good times. But I couldn't remember anything good. I was cut off from my own past, stuck in a hole where before and after no longer seemed to exist. I was like a deer caught in the headlights, paralyzed and aware of nothing but the imminent danger staring me in the face.

In May 1973, more than a year before, Ulrike had written about her experiences in the Dead Wing: "The person sitting in the Dead Wing is unable, even at the beginning, to tell precisely, specifically, certainly what is going on and deludes even himself about the extent and the progress of his own destruction, especially as the thing annihilates his ability to think coherently and creatively, as if hacking at his thoughts with an axe, and he is constantly running after the debris."

As I wasn't even aware of what the Dead Wing was doing to me, I was, of course, unable to communicate it to the others. As a result, nobody felt it necessary to start a public campaign against the Dead Wing in Lübeck, the way they had against the Dead Wing in Cologne, when Astrid Proll, Ulrike Meinhof, and Gudrun Ensslin were there, or for Ronald Augustin in Celle. In my desperate attempt to understand this reality and to try to make the others understand the situation I was in, I described the Dead Wing in all its details, drawing it out on a piece of paper. The only response came from Gudrun, a perfunctory "Good, so we've seen that now." I felt terribly abandoned.

When we were arrested in February, a discussion was already taking place in *Info* about the need to go on a collective hunger strike in an attempt to have the prison conditions changed. This discussion, based on the certainty that years of solitary confinement would break most of us and destroy the collective, continued throughout the summer. We "talked" about the fact that it would be a long and difficult struggle, during which some prisoners might die. It was clear that the state apparatus would regard many prisoners participating in a drawn-out hunger strike to be a challenge to its power and would not give in easily. Each and every one of us would have to be clear about the consequences before deciding. Only those who were prepared to lay their lives down in this struggle should take part. We talked about our experiences during previous smaller hunger strikes and how we wanted to respond to the upcoming longer one. For example, what if one of the prisoners was refused water—would the others then immediately go on thirst strike? The smokers were to try to give up smoking before they started, because cigarettes deprive the body of calcium, which already begins to break down in the bone tissue after a short period on hunger strike.

On September 10, 1974, the trial of Ulrike and others for freeing Andreas three years earlier began in West Berlin. On September 13, Ulrike issued a hunger strike statement in court. This prompted forty prisoners to begin a collective hunger strike. Other prisoners would periodically join the strike, which was to last five months. The principal demands were the abolition of solitary confinement and equal treatment with other prisoners.

Christa Eckes, who had been arrested at the same time as me, and who had been in the main building of Lübeck's women's prison ever since, was placed in the cell next to mine because of the strike. We were allowed to exercise in the yard together for an hour each day. However, the failures during the time we had shared together on the outside weighed heavily on us. In the context of the harsh prison conditions and the challenges of the hunger strike—something new to both of us, at the time—we were simply unable to get past these negative feelings. An additional factor was the state I was in. The end result was that we really rubbed each other the wrong way, and Christa observed my breakdown with suspicion.

I had real difficulties with the thought of going without food. In solitary confinement, food was one of the few things that gave me life. I could touch food, it was something sensual, and it made me able to feel my own existence. I hesitated. I wanted this strike. I was using it to fight desperately for my own survival, and we had no other option. But I was also scared of it. When we started the strike, we had to get rid of our last food items from the canteen. I kept my jam on a shelf in the corner as a secret something I could fall back on. Christa discovered it and got really angry, telling everybody about it in *Info*. She wrote that it was a sign of my dishonesty and unwillingness to fight. I felt so ashamed I wished the earth would open up and swallow me.

The first days without eating were hard. My stomach demanded food, and the hunger made everything else pale in significance. I was unable to think of anything but eating. Even the dreadful Lübeck prison food suddenly smelled appetizing whenever they brought it to our cell doors. It was impossible to read or write, and the hours dragged on endlessly. However, after three or four days, your body adjusts to the new situation. The feeling of hunger subsides, your stomach calms down. The rosehip tea they served us always tasted terrible, with or without sweetener, and its unpleasant furry taste did not leave my mouth until the end of the strike. In the first days, your body refuses any kind of effort, your muscles tremble and don't want to work. But then my body accepted the new diet, and I was able to resume my exercises, almost in the same way as before. It is important not to demand too much of yourself and to drink a great deal, even when you don't feel thirsty.

After about a month on hunger strike, we were brought to Hamburg's remand prison, because Lübeck didn't have facilities for force-feeding at that time. As soon as we arrived in Hamburg, I became keenly aware of the fact that I had been in a Dead Wing at Lübeck. The sudden noises, the presence of so many people, normal prison life—even though very restricted—made me feel hyper. My blood felt as if it was electrified, and I was filled with a great sense of euphoria. For three days and three nights, I was unable to sleep, and then I broke down again. The realization that I had actually been in a Dead Wing came too late to help me defend myself against the effects of months of total isolation.

Irmgard Möller and Ilse Stachowiak were in Hamburg's women's prison at that time; Inga Hochstein got there later. We could see each other during our exercise periods, because our cells all faced the yard. But we didn't have any recreation time together and, from our cells, we couldn't talk to one another. It was clear to everyone that I was teetering on the brink, wavering, and this earned me severe criticism in *Info*. However, I was too far gone to be able to defend myself, or even to get involved in discussions. I reacted by being even more afraid, withdrawing further into myself. After that, I was removed from the *Info* distribution list.

My pride was hurt, but I went along with it. My removal from the list brought with it a sense of relief: I no longer had to force myself to deal with the discussions, something I didn't feel able to do anyway, and I was finally free from the immense pressure this had put on me.

After six weeks on hunger strike, force-feeding began in Hamburg, as it already had in other prisons. A squad of about six guards came into my cell and dragged me off violently to a basement. A prison doctor was waiting with a tube in the cell they had prepared especially for this purpose. The guards violently shoved me onto a kind of dentist's chair, holding down my arms and legs. When they were unable to insert the tube in my nose, they tried to pry open my mouth with a piece of wood so that they could force the tube down my throat. If they succeeded, a nutritional fluid would then be pumped rapidly into my stomach. The other prisoners received the same treatment, the procedure being carried out every two days or even daily. Every time they did it, it was like being raped. Afterward, I would lay for hours on my cot, shattered and unable to think, while I listened to the screams of the others who were being similarly humiliated.

In the newspapers and on the radio and television, there were daily reports about the hunger strike, reports that were full of lies and threats. They gave the impression that the hunger strike was some kind of attack by the guerrilla, as if it were a kidnapping or an armed occupation. The reports never said anything about the prison conditions but always denounced our struggle, denying our humanity. They said we were eating, and that life in our cells was better than how people lived on the outside. They said we thought we were better than regular prisoners, that we were selfish, violent, obsessed with power, immoral, and dangerous. They also said we were not fighting to improve prison conditions, which were already excellent, but that we were campaigning for a continuation of the armed struggle and the destruction of democracy. It was always the same journalists who reported about us, and they contradicted themselves all the time. The aim was simply to keep the press campaign going at full speed, using any arguments they could come up with. I listened to and read all of this, and it took its toll on me, making me feel vulnerable and defenseless. "Doesn't anybody realize they're lying?" I wondered, sadly. "Do people have such short memories that they can't remember what they were told two weeks ago?"

As the weeks wore on, it gradually became clear to me that the hunger strike would not succeed in having solitary confinement abolished and us integrated into regular prison life. When I had begun the hunger strike, focusing on these goals had helped me survive. Solitary confinement was killing me, and I wanted, with all of the strength I had left, to get out of there. The more I doubted that the hunger strike would achieve this, the more my commitment faltered.

One day, I was lying on my cot, shattered and humiliated as always by the force-feeding, when my cell door flew open and my mother was suddenly standing next to me. The last time I had seen her was in 1971, before my first arrest, and I had refused to have any contact with her since. And here she was standing in my cell crying and begging me, "You're my daughter, and I don't want you to die, there's so much left to live for." I was incapable of reacting. Her sobbing moved me, but I said nothing, and she just stood there weeping silently. After a few minutes, the guards took her out of the cell.

I was absolutely furious at this shameless tactic. There was a special section of the prison for visitors outside of the main cell block, and visits never occurred without the supervision of at least a guard or a cop. And now they had brought my mother to my cell. I should have thrown her out, but that never occurred to me. I was immediately consumed by feelings of guilt. Why did I have the wrong reaction? Why had I not thrown her out and ruined this State Security trick? Other than prison employees and the pigs, nobody had entered any of our cells. Not even when Holger was on his deathbed and unable to walk was his lawyer permitted to visit him in his cell. Instead, they had brought him to the visitors' room on a stretcher. Yet they had brought my mother to my cell in the hope that this would induce me to end my hunger strike.

Holger died on November 9, 1974. It was clear to us that the government had killed him deliberately with their force-feeding methods.

Holger had been brutally force-fed 400 to 800 calories every day. However, an adult needs at least 1,200 to 1,600 calories a day to survive. The number of calories your body is given daily is a decisive factor in force-feeding. If it is less than what your body needs, you will lose weight more quickly than you would on a hunger strike with no calories at all, as was the case with Holger.

The following week, *Stern* magazine published a two-page photo of Holger's dead body, starved to a mere skeleton. His death and this photo both horrified and frightened me.

We all took Holger's death to mean that the government would never give in to our demand to abolish solitary confinement, no matter what the price. This realization led the hunger strikers to issue a new demand: that they be brought together in groups, to at least put an end to individual solitary confinement. We wanted to be put into groups with our comrades—with other political prisoners—something that was a matter of course in most countries. We would be separated from the other prisoners but would have contact with one another and could lead some kind of life together, even if strictly controlled. However, the Federal Republic had its own ideas about "the perfect solution"—the German model.

After two months of hunger strike and force-feeding and having realized that the government was not going to abolish solitary confinement, I broke off my hunger strike, unable to continue. A few days before me, Gerhard Müller, who had been arrested in 1972, and who was also imprisoned in Hamburg, had also broken off his strike. The fact that we had stopped striking was featured that evening on the news. It was broadcast as a sign that the hunger strike was crumbling and could be expected to end soon.

Gerhard tried to contact me via the prison doctor, but I refused to have anything to do with him. I didn't want to join up with someone else on the basis of defeat. The other prisoners who were continuing their hunger strike were absolutely furious with me, accusing me of having weakened their cause. Using me as an example, it could now be argued that the hunger strike was falling apart. In the eyes of the others, I was a traitor to the political struggle who might even be willing to cooperate with the police.

That thought never occurred to me, not for a second. It is true, however, that Gerhard began denouncing his former comrades, and I soon learned that he had fired his defense lawyer and had started talking to the BKA. He made statements against his former comrades and managed to make a deal with the Office of the Federal Prosecutor that the murder charge for shooting and killing policeman Schmid in Hamburg would be dropped in exchange for his appearing at various RAF trials as a crown witness.

I began eating again, but I didn't feel good about it. When the time came for them to bring lunch or the evening meal, the guards would shout along the whole length of the corridor, "Meal for Schiller!" This went on every day for three months. Inga Hochstein, who had been arrested during the hunger strike, and who had joined it immediately, as well as Christa, Irmgard, and Ilsa, could all hear this, which was, indeed, the whole point. And every day, I listened as the four women were dragged off to be force-fed. Every day, I watched them get thinner and weaker. I didn't know what to do anymore; I felt completely paralyzed. There was no point in resuming my hunger strike, as I knew I wouldn't be able to keep it up, yet I wanted nothing more than to do so. Some of the guards and the prison director Heinemann tried to talk to me and establish some kind of rapport, a tactic that had also been used during my first period in prison in 1972. I had been criticized for this in the 4.2 Group but had refused to accept this criticism. Now the confrontation had become so intense, what with the Lübeck Dead Wing and the hunger strike, that there was no room for shades of grey. It became vital to my sense of self-respect to close myself off to everything that had to do with the courts and the state apparatus.

Heinemann had been in charge of the goons who had dragged us to be force-fed. It was the guards who had locked the doors after these torture sessions. Now they were offering me the chance to be moved to another floor away from the hunger strikers. I emphatically refused.

Meanwhile, on the outside, a new RAF group had formed since our arrest, and they issued a short statement in which they appealed to the prisoners to break off their hunger strike: "We are asking you to call off your hunger strike now even though the demand for an end to isolation has not been met. ... We are taking this weapon away from you, because the prisoners' struggle—given the existing balance of power—is now something that we must settle with our weapons."

After five months, the others broke off their hunger strike on February 2, 1975, without having achieved anything.

There had been a great deal of support for the prisoners' demands during the strike. I was barely aware of this in my own fight to retain my sense of self; I had been too focused on my own situation. As a result, I can't say much about it, but I do know that after Holger's death there were demonstrations everywhere, even in very small towns. In many places, there was intense street fighting, and a demonstration in West Berlin drew more than fifteen thousand people. The day after Holger's death, the 2nd of June Movement tried to kidnap Günter von Drenkmann, the president of the West Berlin Supreme Court, from his home, shooting him dead when he resisted.

Even before the hunger strike started, there had been widespread public protests in Europe against the political prisoners' conditions and against isolation torture. Jean-Paul Sartre had visited Andreas in Stammheim, on December 4, 1974, during the strike. In France, Italy, and other countries, intellectuals and left-wing groups protested the German state's efforts to destroy the prisoners from the guerrilla.

The conditions for political prisoners in Germany were an important reference point in many political discussions and activities.

Even all of this was not enough. West Germany had joined the US in taking a leading role in the fight against the revolutionary movements in all the NATO states. And then it happened again—in December a bomb exploded in a locker at Bremen's main railway station. Müller, who was now cooperating with State Security, claimed the attack had been carried out by the RAF. I, on the other hand, had no doubt: after the threat of bombs in Stuttgart's city center and the claims about SAM-7 missiles targeting the Volkspark stadium, the state had now gone so far as to actually plant a bomb itself.

During the hunger strike, and even more so afterward, the police and prison guards were just waiting for things to blow up between me and the other four women. A little over three weeks after the end of the collective hunger strike, I was exercising in the yard when Irmgard Möller appeared at the window of her cell and, using our finger language, asked if I wanted to spend my recreation period with her and talk. I nodded. After finishing my yard time, I asked to be brought to Irmgard's cell. It was Friday afternoon, and they told me that permission for a recreation period hadn't been submitted in my case, and the judge responsible for making such decisions had gone home for the weekend, so I would have to wait until Monday.

Over the previous weeks, the total isolation had been relaxed for the hunger-striking women, and they were allowed to get together in their cells two at a time. During the hunger strike, this decision had had a supervisory function, as the women's lives were in danger, and it was to be assumed that they might collapse or fall into a coma at any time. It made the guards' work easier if the prisoners were not alone, otherwise they would have had to sit in the cells with them twenty-four hours a day to make sure that everything was alright. Because I had broken off my hunger strike earlier than the others, this decision didn't apply to me, so I had to wait until Monday. When Monday morning came, the first thing I did was to request recreation time with Irmgard. They brought me to the yard, and I was able to go to her. We hugged, but before either one of us could say a word, the door opened.

"Frau Schiller, pack your things," the guard said, "You're being transferred to Lübeck."

Sensory Deprivation

State Security had waited hoping the others would turn on me after the hunger strike ended. When they saw that this was not going to happen, the only option they could come up with was to simply finish me off.

On the way to Lübeck, I wondered where they would put me now. I was sure that I would be placed in the main prison building this time, maybe even with normal prison conditions. When we arrived in Lübeck, however, they led me directly to the Dead Wing. There could be no doubt about it: they wanted to squeeze what life I had left out of me. This time, though, I knew what their intentions were and was already familiar with the form of torture they planned to use against me. I was now in a position to consciously defend myself and to fight and possibly win back some of what I had lost.

At the same time as my transfer back to Lübeck, the courts decided that my relatives were allowed to visit me. During my entire time in prison, this had been disallowed, and the motivation for the change was as clear as that for my transfer. They were trying to make it impossible for me to focus on political matters; they wanted to get me to revert back to my old, pre-political self.

I thought about my situation and decided to accept visits from my parents, my brother, and my sister. Ever since that day, when the BKA had sent my mother into my cell during the hunger strike and I hadn't thrown her out, I had felt the need to once again have things out with my family. I wrote my mother nasty, insulting letters, and when she visited anger welled up inside me as I watched my parents smiling at the guards and the supervising police team, seeking their confirmation that the conditions I was subjected to were not as bad as I described.

On their second visit, my father told me how I was now totally alone, that there was nobody who wanted to help me anymore, and so, therefore, I needed them. My parents' attitude and what they said confirmed what I already suspected: there wasn't even the slightest basis for dialogue between us. They still wanted to treat me like a child who did not have the right to make her own decisions and whose ideas they were not bound to respect. I ended the visit after five minutes and refused to have any further contact with them. The situation with my sister was more or less the same.

I was then able to have the talk I had been wanting to have with my brother. He had resumed his business economics studies and was just finishing his degree. He didn't like it, but it was what he knew. He spoke more slowly and deliberately, and I felt it was as if a part of him was missing.

Our discussions returned to the same subject again and again—the fact that we are all responsible for our own lives. I was responsible for myself and for my past, for my decisions and my mistakes—and our parents bore responsibility for their past, for what had happened in Germany, for the consequences of their actions or their failures to act. We discussed the dynamics within our family, our upbringing. When it came down to it, my mother had always taken a subordinate role to my father, doing nothing when he threatened us with violence or when he actually used violence against us. In those situations, she was never on our side. The most that she dared to do was to show solidarity with us secretly in our bedrooms. We spoke about the fact that our parents were a product of their times, walking a thin line between societal constraints and individual will, but nonetheless still responsible for their actions, just as we were for ours.

In late February 1975, around the time I was transferred back to Lübeck, the 2nd of June Movement kidnapped Peter Lorenz, the head of the West Berlin CDU, winning the liberation of five prisoners, who were flown to South Yemen.

I was listening to the radio one evening, in late April 1975, when I heard the news that the German Embassy in Stockholm had been seized by the Holger Meins Commando. Over the next few hours, I learned from the newspapers and the radio that this RAF unit was occupying the embassy to demand the release of twenty-six prisoners, who were to be flown out of the country. To my great surprise, my name was on the list.

The commando had shot and killed two embassy staff to show that they were serious. Then, twelve hours into the operation, some of the explosives planted by the unit detonated. The explosion had not been triggered by the commando itself but presumably from the outside. Ulrich Wessel was killed in the explosion, and Siegfried Hausner suffered life-threatening burns that required specialist medical treatment. Despite protests by the Swedish doctor who was treating him, the German government exerted pressure to have him brought to Stammheim prison, instead of to a hospital, where he died eleven days later, without receiving medical care.

I knew all of the members of the Holger Meins Commando, some from my time in the SPK, and others from my time in Hamburg following my first release from prison. Ulrich Wessel was a very decent, meticulous, and considerate person. Siegfried was more like the opposite. When I met him for the first time in the SPK, he was about seventeen years old, angry and hyped up, just having run away from home.

The operation had failed. The comrades were all either dead or captured. I wouldn't have wanted to carry out this operation myself, but it still gave me courage. "Outside," the world beyond the prison walls, existed once again for me. I no longer felt buried behind those walls, beyond any echo of life.

Saigon, the capital city of South Vietnam, fell—all of the newspapers carried photos of the collaborators who had been left behind trying to hang on to the last American helicopters as they evacuated. I cheered at this long war having finally come to an end and at the defeat of US imperialism. I also studied the literature I had on the states that had just achieved independence from Portugal—Angola, Mozambique, and Guinea-Bissau. A great deal of material on this subject had accumulated in my cell: newspapers, books, collections of articles. I saw once again how the history of five hundred years of colonialism was always the same at its core. The European colonial powers maintained that they had brought civilization to the "savages," but the reality was completely different. In Guinea-Bissau, in 1960, the main export was peanuts and the main import alcohol, and 99 percent of the population was illiterate. The Europeans didn't give a damn about the people there, yet Portugal had sent forty thousand soldiers to this small country after the liberation struggle began in the 1960s. I read and read, and a feeling of hate once again welled up within me, a desire to do something about the misery in the Third World. I ordered an atlas so that I could get as exact a picture as possible of these countries. We had been given permission by the courts to use a record player, and I listened to songs from Angola and Guinea-Bissau. I loved the rhythm, the deep voices, and the sad melodies, and I tried to sing along with them, even though I couldn't speak Portuguese. I had a Portuguese language course sent to me and began learning, but it was hopeless. The words I heard seemed to have nothing to do with what was written on the page, and I didn't even know how to move my mouth to make the necessary sounds. I looked at the record and book covers, at the Black people's faces and the beauty of the landscape; I would have loved to have traveled there. Over and over again, I listened to their music, just as I listened to the sad songs from Chile that brought tears to my eyes.

Once again, I remained alone in the Dead Wing for just under six months. *Info* no longer existed, its distribution having been rendered impossible in early 1975 by a gamut of changes to the law, generally referred to as the Lex Baader-Meinhof, or Baader-Meinhof Laws, which restricted the activities of defense lawyers. From time to time, however, my lawyer would bring me a short letter from the Hamburg women, in which they would tell me what they were currently working on and ask what I was up to.

I read about Hamburg psychiatrist Jan Gross's research on sensory deprivation at the Eppendorf University Clinic, i.e., on the deprivation of all sensory stimuli and the opportunities this presented for manipulating people. This research clearly had something to do with our prison conditions. West Germany and the US were leaders in this field and in implementing the findings in the architectural design of their prisons. I tried to get a hold of material on the effects of isolation, so that I could better understand what had happened to me in the Dead Wing and what it was I now had to prepare for.

While I already knew more about what was being inflicted on me this time, that didn't stop total isolation from taking its toll. I was always cold, even though it was summer. I felt a weight on my chest that made it difficult for me to breathe; I became convinced that I had lung cancer. The pressure in my ears never stopped. Any kind of physical exercise required a great deal of effort, as did reading even a single page. I had to summon up all of my inner resources to stop myself from sinking into mood swings, ranging from listlessness to intense aggressiveness.

One day, I received a bright blue scarf; as soon as I saw the color tears came to my eyes, the clear, intense blue stirring up deep emotions. In the cell and in the Dead Wing, every-thing was white, gray, or washed-out green, and the guards' uniforms were dark blue. Lively colors were as rare as lively sounds.

After five or six months alone in the Dead Wing, they brought Christa back again. We both recalled how things had been between us the year before; this time, being with her helped me to understand reactions that were a product of the isolation and to notice things with her that I had also noticed in myself, without having previously understood their cause. I was greatly relieved to hear that the other pris-oners often felt the same way.

Small things could take on terrifying dimensions when you were alone in your cell, if you didn't find some way to laugh about them and to deal with them calmly. After the long time spent on hunger strike, it was impossible for me to store food in my cell. I gobbled every single thing I bought weekly at the canteen the very day I got it. When I received Helma's birthday parcel full of sweets, I stuffed myself with those treasures non-stop for two days, until I felt sick. On the third day, I threw all that was left down the toilet, because I didn't know what else to do. I judged myself for completely lacking in discipline, criticized my loss of self-control, and regarded this as a sign of the collapse of my political iden-tity. When Christa arrived, she told me that all of the other political prisoners in Hamburg felt the same way and had, therefore, stored all the food they had in Christa's cell, as she was the only one of them who had suffered from the oppo-site problem since the strike, hardly eating anything at all. When I heard this, I was so relieved I wasn't alone in what I was going through that tears came to my eyes, and I couldn't stop grinning.

We read the newspapers together every day, discussing their contents. The trial of Gudrun, Ulrike, Jan-Carl, and Andreas in Stammheim had begun at the end of May 1975.

By making a series of changes to the law, the government had begun preparations for the trial in late 1974, while the accused were still on hunger strike. It was now forbidden for the accused to share a lawyer; Paragraph 129 stipulating that each defendant must have their own counsel. But there weren't that many lawyers willing to defend us in the face of the enormous public animosity. What's more, trials could now be conducted in the absence of the defendants. The law proceeded from the assumption that "hunger strikes were used to induce a state of unfitness for trial." Before the trial began, Andreas's three defense lawyers Klaus Croissant, Christian Ströbele, and Kurt Groenewold, who had visited us the longest in prison, and who knew the most about our prison conditions, as well as being the most familiar with the trial documents, were barred from court. Attorney General Buback accused them of being "mouthpieces" and "members of the same criminal organization as their clients," because they used the "terminology of left extremism, such as isolation torture, extermination conditions, brainwashing units, and the like."

The trial took place in a bunker that had been built especially for that purpose, a concrete symbol of the methods the state apparatus intended to use to vanquish the RAF phenomenon. A flood of newspaper articles about this show trial poured into our cells, great efforts being made to stand reality on its head. Every single motion concerning prison conditions was regarded as an attempt to delay the proceedings, and the four defendants were made out to be demonic broken monsters. The Springer Corporation's *Die Welt* newspaper put it succinctly: "Every attempt to humanize the terrorists is irresponsible and stupid."

Christa and I studied the petitions from the lawyers and the four comrades in the Stammheim trial, and we looked for any information we could find on their prison conditions and the use of isolation torture. While doing so, we came across an explanation for something we had already experienced ourselves. After years in total isolation, putting two people together intensifies the effects of the isolation. We started making an effort to keep this new piece of information in mind in our day-to-day dealings with one another. For a time, we succeeded.

The trial was accompanied by sensationalist news stories claiming that the RAF had stolen mustard gas and intended to pollute Lake Constance with nuclear waste. In September, a bomb exploded in Hamburg's central train station. Christa and I tried to make a list of all of the threats and actions of this type that had occurred since the beginning of the armed struggle in West Germany. We had already spent some time reading books from counterinsurgency specialists and former CIA agents, so we knew that campaigns of this sort were typical of the methods used by secret services. The aim was to break down solidarity, spread fear, cause insecurity. For those defending the existing order, these were critical battlegrounds. "Normal citizens" were meant to think that they could be the next victim, that the guerrillas didn't give a damn about the lives of the general public.

After four or six weeks together in the Dead Wing, Christa and I were transferred to Hamburg, where the trial of the 4.2 Group was set to begin in November.

A Death and a Death Threat

Our transfer to Hamburg brought the surprising news that two of us could now share a single cell. Two medical experts had found that Irmgard Möller would not be fit to stand trial if something didn't change immediately regarding her isolation conditions. We were excited. We had spent such a long time in total isolation, the only small improvement being that recently we had been allowed to spend one or two hours a day together during recreation. With this complete suspension of isolation, it now seemed like our torture was finally over.

I moved into a cell with Christa, and Irmgard moved in with Ilse Stachowiak—and so it was that we fell into a new trap. From that point on, it was no longer possible for any of us to ever be alone, not even for a short time. After having been constantly alone, this absolute reversal of the situation was unbearable and led to a great deal of emotional tension. The first to break under this great stress was me. After a short time, I became fixated on every movement Christa made in the cell, watching her constantly. I was unable to think or do anything for myself. Just as incapable of bearing the situation, Christa reacted with hostility and rejection. Neither of us had any space to breathe.

After a little less than a month, I applied to be transferred back to a cell of my own. From that point on, things got even worse. I could no longer read or write, and for more than a year I was unable to formulate a complete sentence.

The other three women could no longer help me, as they had to fight for themselves. They didn't spend recreation time with me anymore. Only rarely did one of them come into my cell to see if anything had changed in my numbed state. Confronted with my helplessness, which they could do nothing about, they always left my cell again after just a few minutes.

Inga was the only one who joined me in the yard. She had never been a RAF member nor was she a part of any other organization.

Alone in my cell, I paced back and forth for hours on end. Two steps from one side to the other. Four large or six normal steps from the door to the window. I had no idea how long I could keep this up. All that mattered was that I make it to the next morning. I tried reading a book, but gave up after one paragraph, as I couldn't understand what I was reading. Sometimes, a sentence found its way through to me, one from the torture camps in Vietnam, for example, and this gave me the feeling of being alive, and that I would somehow make my way back to the surface. But then I became numb again.

My "adoptive mother" Helma had been active in the group of family members who had some respect for the guerrilla struggle and for the political prisoners. They would meet together regularly, even if they didn't all share the same political convictions, but since I had broken off my hunger strike Helma had been having problems in the group. I was no longer capable of responding to what was going on around me, the situation had become too intense, so I burned my last bridge and broke off my last remaining contact with the outside. I told Helma that she should stop visiting and writing to me.

The state apparatus was escalating its fight against the prisoners from the guerrilla, the hunger strike and Holger's death had shown everyone how fierce the confrontation had become, and the Stammheim trial was now underway. In this context, discussions in the solidarity groups about the right way forward became increasingly intense, a process that would come to a head in 1977. The courts often barred visitors. We were to be cut off from political discussions as much as possible, and nobody on the outside was to be allowed to get to know us anymore, so that the psychological warfare campaign describing us as hard, insensitive, politically naive, and selfish gangsters could proceed unchallenged.

My teeth went to hell, one after the other. I had been born shortly after the war, which meant that I had always had a calcium deficiency and was lacking in other elements required to develop strong bones and teeth. In prison, I was once again failing to get what I needed. I got no sun, and the food I ate was deficient in vitamins and minerals. The dentist only came when absolutely necessary. At the end of December 1975, I was in terrible pain. My gums had peeled away from the nerve on one of my back teeth, leaving it exposed. I could hardly eat or even drink anything, it didn't matter if it was warm or cold, and every breath of air hurt like hell. The prison dentist happened to be on holiday. I thought my head was going to explode from the pain, and there was nothing in the cell to distract me. Nothing but me and my pain. Ten days seemed like an eternity—then, all of a sudden, the pain stopped. Was the nerve dead? I didn't know. But since then, I have never again had a toothache. My subconscious will not allow that kind of pain to get through to my conscious mind anymore. Since then, I have also endured every single dental treatment without anesthetic.

There were heated disagreements between the lawyers and the RAF prisoners about what strategy to pursue at the various trials that were to be held in 1975. Most of the prisoners wanted to concentrate all their efforts on Stammheim. It was there that the state apparatus was bringing to bear its heaviest ammunition, it was there that there would be the most press coverage, and it was there that the RAF founders were being tried. This discussion had also become necessary because of the newly introduced regulation that stopped a lawyer from representing more than one defendant.

The trial of those of us who had been arrested on February 4, 1974, was due to begin in November 1975. Because of the state we were in, we had little interest in participating in any trial at all. In any case, I didn't participate in these discussions, and I wasn't interested in the trial. It was clear to me that the judgment would be political and would be determined by the selection of the judges, the choice of public prosecutors, and the way in which the charges had been formulated. I definitely didn't want to be ripped apart in the press again, as I had been constantly since 1971. The chief judge was the same one who had presided over my first trial—Ziegler. He wasn't one of those hell-bent on setting an example, seeing themselves as serving a "democracy" at war. The charges were mainly collective ones, and there weren't any specific charges against me as an individual. Unlike Stammheim, nobody expected a terror verdict in our case.

When the trial finally began in early 1976, Helmut, Wolfgang, Ilse, and Christa presented a joint statement. Eberhard and I sat looking on apathetically. Eberhard had distanced himself from the others some time ago, and Kay had been released from prison because of a life-threatening illness. After that, we got ourselves expelled from the proceedings by making a racket and refusing to sit down. At the same time, we fired the defense lawyers we trusted, so that they would not be forced to conduct the case without us. That left only the court-appointed counsel, whom we called the "imposed counsel." The Stammheim trial had begun with the introduction of "defense lawyers" the defendants did not trust. This was so that after they had rejected all of the lawyers we trusted, the trial could proceed without the defendants having any real representation. Ulrike, Andreas, Gudrun, and Jan wanted to defend themselves, and the government tried to do everything it could to prevent this. We didn't want to defend ourselves, but we did want to at least make it clear what the recent changes in the law implied, i.e., a meaningless trial in which the defendants were not represented in any real way. The imposed counsel had been chosen by the court without our consent and were paid by the state. We refused to speak a single word to them during the entire trial, which lasted eight months.

On May 9, as always, I was sitting alone in my cell listening to the radio, when the program was suddenly interrupted. The news anchor announced that Ulrike Meinhof had been found dead in her cell that morning, that she had committed suicide. Everything in me seized up, my heart began to pound uncontrollably, and even my watch stopped ticking, as my body's entire magnetic field changed. My mind was racing: What had happened? Suicide? Could that be possible? Ulrike? As so often before, I knelt at my bedside, leaning my elbows and upper body on the mattress, trying to bring some order to my thoughts. Suicide? I had felt dreadful for months, but I had always rejected any thought of suicide. It seemed to me that if I killed myself I would be abandoning my life to the state and the media; I would be giving them a chance to exploit the situation, to prey on me, as they always saw suicide as an act of despair to use against the comrades. Even if I no longer knew how to continue the fight, I did not want to give them a gift like that. Had Ulrike decided otherwise?

I just couldn't believe it. They had never managed to shut her up; right to the end, she had always fought for everything. I knew that there had been serious conflicts over the past year between Gudrun and Ulrike. However, that was also part of the struggle to survive under the conditions of long-term isolation, which is designed to create aggression, as I myself had experienced, and both Gudrun and Ulrike were very passionate. I could have imagined her falling silent, but that is not what had happened.

The Stammheim trial was about to enter a critical phase. While the court was reviewing the evidence, the four prisoners were working hard on their statements about Vietnam and the RAF's attacks against the US military bases in Heidelberg and Frankfurt in 1972. Ulrike was actively involved in this. Despite the many changes to the law to restrict the rights of the defense and despite the constant press barrage against the Stammheim prisoners, this trial had taken on international importance, and Ulrike, Andreas, Gudrun, and Jan had issued many statements. It wasn't like the silence of isolation, where every sentence, every scream went unanswered. During the trial, she could raise her voice, and it had an effect. Why would Ulrike commit suicide at this stage in the proceedings?

I paced back and forth in my cell and thought, "It can only have been murder." Why did they do it? I remembered that the Nazis had murdered the poet Erich Mühsam using the method of "suicide by hanging," a method used throughout the world against political prisoners who refused to break. And now it had happened in the supposedly "democratic" Federal Republic of Germany. It was always their goal to kill the leaders of resistance movements. In Guinea-Bissau, Amilcar Cabral was murdered in 1976, in Mozambique, Mondlane in 1969, Che Guevara in 1967. I thought back to 1972, when they had spread the rumor that Ulrike had committed suicide because of differences within the group.

A few days after her death, as I was pacing up and down in my cell, a guard opened the door and said, "Come with me, you have a visitor." A visitor? I never got visitors, and I didn't correspond with anyone anymore, so who could it be? "Who is it? I'm not expecting anyone, and I'm not leaving my cell if I don't know who it is."

Ten minutes went by, and then my cell door opened again and two officers from the BKA, who I recognized from my first arrest, came in. "Frau Schiller, have you not had enough yet?" one of them asked. This provoked a wave of fury in me. They had been watching as my condition deteriorated day by day. With Ulrike's death, they now thought that I would be completely depleted and would collaborate with them. "Get out!" I screamed, looking for the nearest thing I could find to throw at them as they fled from my cell.

From that point on, I started to feel better. I once again saw clearly the effect the prison conditions they had imposed were meant to have on us. I also again saw clearly who had ordered them and was using them against me. In isolation, over time, you lose your concept of anything sensual, and that is exactly when the hole in which you lose yourself opens up to swallow you. Because nothing is definite anymore, nothing is tangible. You have nothing but yourself and the walls; anything else you have to get a hold of through your thoughts.

When I told the others that the pigs had been in my cell, they realized that they had made a mistake and had misjudged me. They realized they had abandoned me to State Security and had stopped seeing me as a comrade who needed help. We started spending recreation time together and talking to one another again. We read the Stammheim prisoners' trial statements. We swapped newspapers, and I started once again poring over the news. Among the articles I read, I found interviews with Gerhard Müller about the RAF. He used the press reports about differences within the group after Ulrike's death to pave the way for a deal with the Office of the Federal Prosecutor, which offered to acquit him on the charge of murdering a policeman in exchange for making a statement at Stammheim. I found it obscene how he spoke of Andreas, Gudrun, and the structure of the RAF. None of us from the RAF was the model of "the new human being" nor were we saints. None of us could live up to our own ideas about new kinds of human relationships, and in our day-to-day lives we repeatedly fell into the same traps, but none of that had anything to do with Müller's clichés. We had to do something about this situation. I thought that I could make a statement at Stammheim about the deal he had made. I could provide details about what he was doing with State Security, because I knew that he had been the one who had fired his weapon the night I was arrested in Hamburg. He had been charged for this but not convicted. He had already spilled everything to State Security before the trial began, but it was only after sentencing that he was willing to publicly play the part of crown witness.

I went to Irmgard's cell to tell her what I was considering. She thought it was a good idea and suggested that we inform the Stammheim prisoners via the lawyers and ask what they thought.

There are some details, no matter how small, that you never forget as long as you live. About a week later, on a Friday, my cell door was opened by a guard at 8:00 a.m. She had a letter for me in her hand. It was a sealed white envelope with nothing but my name on it, without an official stamp of any kind. Normally, letters that I received had at least two official stamps, one from the court and one from the prison. What's more, the letters had always been opened and then visibly closed again with an official seal. All of these typical markings were missing. The moment she handed the letter to me, the guard realized this herself. "I have to check if I can give you this letter," she said, taking it back from me, "something's not right."

Half an hour later, I was to be brought to my lawyer. I was escorted along several corridors, up stairways and past barred windows to the part of the building where the cells were. It was here that we normally met with the lawyers. All of a sudden, Gerhard Müller was standing in front of me. I had known him since 1971, as he had also been a member of the SPK. They had brought him to Hamburg to meet with me, possibly to persuade me by this personal encounter not to make a statement against him. I pushed him aside and went to my lawyer, telling her about what had just happened.

After about forty-five minutes, I returned to my cell. Five minutes later, the same guard brought me the letter she had had that morning. The letter was still unopened and unstamped. It was a letter from Müller that State Security had had delivered to me with no verification whatsoever.

In the letter, Müller started by reminding me of our common history in the SPK and saying that he had always found me attractive. He then blamed me for the failure of the group that had been arrested in February 1974. He said that I also bore political responsibility for the group, even in prison, and that it was my job to put an end to their illusions by ending the struggle. Finally, he threatened that I would suffer the same fate as Ulrike if I did anything to cross him.

This was a direct death threat if I decided to speak out against Müller. The only way they could have known I was planning to do so was by bugging my cell. I immediately went to Irmgard's cell with the letter. We decided to quickly put it in a safe place to be used as evidence. Luckily, her lawyer was visiting that very day, and she was able to give it to him.

That same afternoon, June 19, 1976, we heard on the radio that a bomb attack had been carried out against the office of my court-appointed attorney, killing one office employee. As far as we were concerned, this had to be a State Security action. My cell was ransacked while I was in the yard—State Security was looking for the letter from Müller. It became clear to us all that I could no longer remain alone.

I moved back into a cell with Christa; Irmgard and Ilsa had remained together throughout this whole time.

I didn't hesitate for even a minute about testifying at Stammheim. In view of these events, I was convinced that it was the right thing to do. First, I drafted a written statement about what had happened during the shooting on the night of October 21–22, 1971. This was to be the basis of a motion by the lawyers to have me called as a witness in Stammheim. Jan asked if I also wanted to say something about Holger and my experiences with him. I tried to put something down on paper but without success. Holger had been important to me, but I could no longer picture him the way he was when he was alive. I couldn't think of anything good to say about the time before my first arrest, and I couldn't remember anything particular that had happened. Everything had become abstract and cut off from me. The fact that my time in isolation had left me unable to remember things hurt and made me feel unsure of myself.

In late July, I was flown to Stuttgart by helicopter. I hated these large, noisy machines that the German border police used, where I sat squeezed in between two BKA officers. The noise from the rotors and the way it shook made me airsick. When we arrived at Stammheim, they brought me to the first or second floor of one of the large modern concrete blocks. All of the prisoners and guards I saw were men. The windows were covered with screens of some sort, making it impossible to see outside. So this is where Ulrike was killed, I thought to myself, as I was overcome by a feeling of great anxiety. This was where the trial of Andreas, Gudrun, and Jan was being conducted, and it was here that I was to make my statement the following day. I called out a window, "Gudrun!" No answer. I shouted louder, "Andreas, Gudrun, Jan!" A prisoner I didn't know called back, saying that they weren't in that wing, so they couldn't hear me. However, Helmut Pohl was somewhere nearby. He had also been flown to Stammheim that same day and was also supposed to make a statement. We were able to communicate by shouting to one another. He was taken in before me, and when he came back he called to me, "I can't remember what I said, I think I talked a load of shit. That bunker and the whole situation completely freaks you out!"

They took me to the "bunker" next, which is what every-body called the building that had been built especially for this trial. After waiting briefly in a small windowless cell in the basement, I was taken upstairs and suddenly found myself under glaring lights on a large stage. The judges' benches were at the top end, to my right there were benches for the lawyers and the prisoners, and the federal prosecu-tors sat at the back and to the left. All of the benches had microphones. There were uniforms everywhere. When two guards brought me to the witness stand at the midpoint of the edge of the stage, I saw, as if looking through a haze, a huge gallery below me, where the press and the public were sitting. After the long period of isolation and the helicopter ride, the strain of standing up there and talking into a micro-phone in this public arena was almost too much for me.

Judge Prinzing asked me my name, age, profession, and place of residence. He asked if I was willing to answer questions. I had thought about that beforehand, about the fact that to make my testimony plausible, not as a political statement but as a witness statement, I was going to have to answer some questions. I said I was willing. I concentrated entirely on that night in Heegbarg and began slowly, per-haps even haltingly, but also confidently, to recount what had happened in the course of that evening, without saying that the other woman had been Ulrike Meinhof. This wasn't about her. When I was finished, Prinzing first asked me a few questions about my statement, followed by the lawyers and the federal prosecutors. This didn't take very long, and then the lawyers asked me if I was also prepared to make statements about the structure of the RAF. Gerhard Müller had not only accused the prisoners from the RAF of specific acts, but, what's more, he had also spoken of a supposed hier-archy, as well as brutality and repression within the group, all of which received widespread media coverage. To refute this, Gudrun, Andreas, and Jan had spoken to the lawyers about calling RAF prisoners as witnesses, to give statements in Stammheim about the group's structure. And this is what many of us did, including Helmut Pohl, Irmgard Möller, and Werner Hoppe, who would all sit in this chair, either before or after me. But at that very moment, just when I was called upon, what I wanted to say—the small structure of thoughts that I had put together in my head—disappeared beyond my grasp. I started a sentence and lost my train of thought halfway through. Haltingly, I delivered a few wooden sentences. When Prinzing interrupted, objecting that I was only repeating what Helmut had already said, I could only answer, "The same experience brings about the same results."

At this point, Federal Prosecutor Zeis took the microphone and asked me, with a smug grin on his face, "Can you tell the court: When was the first time you cooperated with the police?" At that exact moment, all microphones were switched off, the federal prosecutors and the court stood up, and it was obvious that none of them wanted to hear my answer to this public accusation that I had collaborated. Overcome with a hatred that swept me off my feet, I could only scream into the din surrounding me, "Pigs!" and then I was led out.

My head and my body were aching, as if I had been beaten with clubs. Humiliated, small, and miserable, I sat in my cell again. I hadn't seen Gudrun, Jan, and Andreas. Since Ulrike's death, they seldom appeared in court. How did they manage to maintain so much initiative in a prison like this, in this bunker, with the constant back and forth between cell and stage, before the full public gallery? They had issued a great many statements during the trial. They constantly came up with new ideas, were always doing something. I tried to picture them as I was waiting to be transported away by helicopter. However, everything that had happened and the prison had built walls between us, walls that I was no longer able to tear down. It was no longer 1971, when I could grin at Andreas with an "oh, get a grip!" when he said something that I thought was stupid. There was no longer that ease and liveliness in our communication, where a look, a gesture, the unspoken and invisible connections to one another, accompanied our words.

Now, everything was cast in concrete.

After a little less than twenty-four hours in Stammheim, I was brought back to Hamburg. Talking and arguing about my statement had given me strength, despite all of our differences, and had made it possible for me to have a more conscious relationship with myself. I could now debate, argue, and laugh with Irmgard, Christa, Ilse, and Inga. We were never allowed to meet together as a group, though. We were only permitted recreation time together in pairs.

When the 4.2 Group was sentenced in late September 1976, we hardly paid any attention to it, as we hadn't taken part in the trial, and the sentences were not particularly severe. At the time, the highest sentence for membership in a criminal organization was five years. Because the court was unable to prove that we had done anything specific and the Office of the Federal Prosecutor had no political interest in making the details of our activity public, we all received prison sentences of between four and five years, which were relatively short in comparison to others. Only Christa would be sentenced to longer, because of the bank robbery. I got four years and three months.

We spent our time talking or reading, especially the texts and critiques that came out of Stammheim. We all had a great number of books, which we swapped with one another, books about changes in the structure of international capital, about the effects of colonialism and imperialism on the countries of the Third World, about new forms of social control in the metropoles, about the structure of consumer society. Many books were published on the activities of the CIA and the American military to suppress opposition in the

US and around the world. The Vietnam War was over, and important agents had left the CIA and were writing about their experiences and various covert activities. The power structure was undergoing changes in the US and, as a result, many documents that had previously been classified were made public. This was a bonanza for us, and we devoured everything we could get our hands on. We felt that much of what we read confirmed the RAF's analysis and practice.

Buback, Ponto, Schleyer

In the winter of 1976–1977, our small group was suddenly torn apart. Christa, Irmgard, and Ilse were transferred to Lübeck, while Inga and I remained in Hamburg. Irmgard was due to be released soon, so why transfer her? Inga and I got together; we didn't want to just accept this move by the courts without putting up a fight. The only thing that seemed to make any sense was for us five women to go on hunger strike.

I hesitated. There had been repeated discussions over the past year among RAF prisoners about the need for a renewed hunger strike, but I was unsure I could face such an ordeal again. Thinking about it scared me. But it was also clear to me that nothing had improved in terms of prison conditions for most of the political prisoners, indeed the opposite was true: they had become stricter, censoring our letters and preventing us from communicating with one another. The isolation, both from the outside and on the inside, had been ramped up. Faced with the question of whether or not we should go on hunger strike the next day to demand that the three women be transferred back from Lübeck to Hamburg, I was unsure, but I nonetheless decided to participate. This wasn't a "big" hunger strike and would not lead to the kind of confrontation that had occurred in 1974. This was about winning a limited goal, and we were only five women.

The three women in Lübeck had come to the same conclusion: hunger strike—so we began. I was overcome by memories of what had happened previously, both before and after I had broken off my hunger strike, but I was able to speak to Inga about this, and so was not alone. I was always freezing, no matter the season, but now it was winter. Constantly feeling cold became unbearable while on hunger strike; my hands and feet were never warm. I shivered, and nothing, not even three pullovers and a blanket, did any good. I felt as if my arms and legs would drop off.

After fourteen days on hunger strike, we managed to have Ilse and Christa transferred back to Hamburg. They transferred Irmgard to Stammheim for the rest of her sentence, but then, instead of releasing her, they served her with a new arrest warrant in connection with the bomb attack on the US Army headquarters in Heidelberg. The only witness for the prosecution was Gerhard Müller.

There had just been a huge demonstration against the Brokdorf nuclear power plant, involving intense clashes with the police. We were surprised at how much opposition there was to the nuclear power plants. Would this provide a new opening for revolutionary struggle? We were happy to learn of such developments, but what political significance did a movement have that only mobilized spontaneously to support a limited and specific goal? Naturally, "reports" had been put out that, since January 1976, the RAF had been planning attacks on nuclear power stations, as well as operations using nuclear materials and chemical and biological weapons.

In early March 1977, *Spiegel* published a cover story about the nuclear scientist Klaus Traube, who had been the target of illegal wiretaps by the Federal Intelligence Service (Bundesnachrichtendiesnt, BND), because he was suspected of being acquainted with someone who had gone underground with a guerrilla group. As a result of this, other illegal wiretaps came to light, including ones that had targeted RAF prisoners, their lawyers, and foreign groups active in West Germany. The media was full of news stories about these revelations. Minister of the Interior Werner Maihofer was made a scapegoat, and there was talk of removing him from office. The fact that we and our lawyers had been bugged was not news to us. We had repeatedly made this public. We were sure the whole thing had been staged. Behind all the hullabaloo, there was a power struggle between political and secret service factions of the state about centralizing the secret services under the Federal Chancellery. In future, both the civil and the military secret services were to be coordinated by the chief of the Chancellery, meaning that the Ministry of the Interior and the Ministry of Defense would have to give up some of their power.

We saw this situation as the ideal opportunity to start another large-scale hunger strike. We reckoned that the government would be at a disadvantage because of the internal power struggles. We also thought that a hunger strike would lead to public discussion of our prison conditions, because the wiretaps targeting us were in the news. This meant there might be a chance of achieving our demand that all political prisoners be placed in larger groups. We began the hunger strike on March 19, 1977.

From one day to the next, anything to do with the actions of the secret services disappeared from the daily headlines. This also indicated that the conflict between the different political factions within the state had been put aside. Maihofer remained in office, and the secret services were not restructured for the time being.

The small hunger strike demanding the return of the women from Lübeck had been a kind of trial run for me, giving me the confidence to join this larger strike. The fact that I was able to speak to Inga every day gave me a new kind of strength. In 1974, I had nobody to talk to about my questions, my doubts, or the humiliation I felt every time they force-fed me. In Hamburg, we now spent our recreation time in pairs. I could speak with one of the other women every day. That is why, later on, I was able to remember this strike much more clearly than any of the others. In the course of the strike,

RAF prisoner Brigitte Asdonk and 2JM prisoner Annerose Reiche, who had been in West Berlin for years, and after that in Lübeck, were transferred to Hamburg. There were now six of us.

Almost three weeks after the start of our hunger strike, on April 7, 1977, Attorney General Siegfried Buback was shot and killed by the RAF's Ulrike Meinhof Commando. As the communiqué explained:

> Buback was directly responsible for the murders of Holger Meins, Siegfried Hausner, and Ulrike Meinhof. In his function as Attorney General—as the central figure connecting and coordinating matters between the justice system and the West German news services, in close cooperation with the CIA and the NATO Security Committee—he stage-managed and directed their murders.

The attack against Buback made me hesitate. Did it make sense to continue the strike under these conditions? Wouldn't they take their revenge now and use the hunger strike to let several of us die, as they had Holger? Yet it soon became clear that the opposite was true, that the attack by the Ulrike Meinhof Commando had actually won us support. As a direct result, the Office of the Federal Prosecutor tried to enforce a Contact Ban on the Stammheim prisoners, something for which there was no legal basis. The Contact Ban meant that nobody was allowed to see the prisoners, not even their lawyers. Three days later, the ban had to be lifted. The hunger striking prisoners collectively responded to the Contact Ban by escalating to a thirst strike, which we only broke off once the Office of the Federal Prosecutor backed down.

We viewed this attempted Contact Ban as a clear and unequivocal death threat against those in Stammheim. In a prison situation where every form of external oversight is removed, the state can do whatever it wants, and nobody can investigate what happened.

On April 20, 1977, exactly one month into the strike, while we were all still in relatively good condition, a regime of particularly brutal force-feeding was started in Hamburg. No other prison was force-feeding prisoners. Every day, a squad of guards stormed into our cells, grabbed us, and dragged us to the basement, almost breaking our bones while force-feeding us. They tore my nasal wall with the end of the tube, they knocked out one of Werner's teeth, and we all had bruises and bleeding lips. However, after every one of these torture sessions, as I lay battered and humiliated in my cell, Inga would come to me and make me go over everything that had transpired. As I recounted what had happened, I would notice how I was able to breathe again. The opportunity to talk about this terrible experience, the opportunity to share it with someone, somehow took away its horror and its power. Although this hunger strike was harder than the one in 1974, as far as the physical confrontation was concerned, it was easier for me, because I wasn't alone.

There were many declarations of support for our demands: from Amnesty International, from lawyers' groups in the US, and from a very wide range of groups and individuals in several European countries.

We finally called off the hunger strike on April 30, when future Attorney General Kurt Rebmann issued a written promise on behalf of the Baden-Württemberg Minister of Justice to place the Stammheim prisoners together in groups. Two days earlier, as expected, the Stammheim court had imposed multiple life sentences on Andreas, Gudrun, and Jan.

It took two months for them to begin fulfilling their promise in Stammheim; in early July, Helmut Pohl, Wolfgang Beer, and Werner Hoppe were transferred there from Hamburg. Ingrid Schubert had been flown there from West Berlin some months before. This meant that the group now consisted of eight prisoners: Irmgard, Gudrun, Ingrid, Andreas, Jan, Helmut, Wolfgang, and Werner. Based on medical studies, our demand had been for a minimum of fifteen prisoners per group. But prior to then, none of us had ever had the chance to work together, laugh together, see each other daily as a group of eight, and do what was important and what was possible within the limits we faced. After only a very short time together, this group in Stammheim became very solid, despite the fact that the seventh floor was a kind of fishbowl in which the prisoners were watched over, observed, and investigated twenty-four hours a day with cameras, microphones, and the ever-present security agents.

On July 30, 1977, a RAF commando unit tried to kidnap Jürgen Ponto, head of the Dresdner Bank. He was shot dead during the operation. In response to his death the state launched an offensive against the prisoners and their last remaining lawyers.

After Ponto was killed, the Stammheim prisoners' group was broken up. Our collective response to this was to immediately go on hunger and thirst strike. That was August 9; three days later, Helmut, Wolfgang, and Werner were transferred back to Hamburg. For all of us, it was the first time that we had started out with a thirst strike. It is the most difficult and the very last thing a prisoner resorts to as an act of resistance. In contrast to a hunger strike, during which you can and should move around, a thirst strike severely limits your ability to move and to think properly from the very first day. My mouth felt like cotton, every single word required an effort, I lost my voice due to dehydration and was only able to whisper incomprehensibly. In this situation, we were barred from recreation, meaning we were hardly able to communicate, as our voices were too weak to call from one cell window to another.

Before our thirst strike, medical science assumed that a person dies after three or four days without food and liquids.

The prison doctors and police scientists looked on in surprise when, on the fifth, sixth, and even seventh day we still managed to walk around the yard. It is true that we walked slowly and with great difficulty, but we walked upright. At first, the guards let us stand under one of the cell windows during our yard time and carry out short discussions using our fingers. To get around the microphones, we had learned a finger language, which we often used to talk to one another in our cells as well. The longer the strike went on, the more they tried to prevent any form of communication between us. We had to exchange our finger messages secretly between the yard and the cell windows, which sometimes only gave us enough time for a few letters per round. Proper communication became nearly impossible.

The state adopted a hard line. The media was full of propaganda, and people who openly expressed solidarity with the hunger strike and protested against our prison conditions could face arrest.

It was a really hard fight. Like almost all the others, I was unable to read. I mostly lay immobile on my bed as time seemed to stand still. On the seventh day of the thirst strike, the Hamburg prison doctors ordered blood samples to be taken by force. This showed that our blood sugar levels and dialysis values were at an absolute minimum, meaning that it would no longer be possible to save someone's life if they dropped any further. All of the prisoners on thirst strike were in a similar state. Two hours later, I was rushed on a gurney right through the entire prison to the sick bay. Once there, they strapped me down to a hospital bed so that I was completely immobilized and put me on an IV drip. I felt every single drop of the infusion flow into my body. For seven hours, I lay there strapped down by my arms, legs, stomach, and chest until my body had been given the intended amount of fluids. I saw them bringing more of us into the sick bay, but we could not communicate with one another.

When, after seven hours, the medical attendant loosened the straps, my entire body began to shake uncontrollably, and I started to sob and could not stop. I had lost all control over my limbs and my nerves. Twelve prisoners were given infusions for a week in Hamburg. The subsequent ones didn't take as long as the first—four or five hours.

The prison clinic was not equipped to deal with so many prisoners in such a condition, so we had to be brought there on gurneys one after another, transported through the whole prison building. When transporting comrades in prison, the guards were always trying to injure us by bumping violently into bars or corners. As special security measures still applied to us, and we were not supposed to see or speak to any other prisoners, all normal prison activities were suspended that week. In Holstenglacis prison, which at that time housed about 1,400 prisoners, hardly any lawyers' visits could take place. During that week, all other visits, as well as the prisoners' yard time, was completely canceled.

To end the paralysis of the prison, the prison doctors decided to adopt another method to administer fluids: using a thick needle, up to one liter of a glucose solution was injected daily into our upper thighs, the process taking an hour each time. This carried with it a direct risk of circulatory collapse, because, for a body as weakened as ours were, it is an enormous strain to absorb such a large quantity of liquid from an intramuscular injection. My legs were so swollen afterward that I couldn't get my pants back on for several hours.

At the same time, our legal advocates were also targeted. Over the previous years, the defense attorneys had been subject to sanctions from the Bar Association's disciplinary committee, as well as criminal proceedings. They had been repeatedly expelled from court, some being barred from practicing law. Their names had been dragged through the mud by the press, and they received death threats. Attorney Klaus Croissant had fled to France when facing arrest for a third time. There were only two lawyers left who we trusted: Armin Newerla and Arndt Müller.

On August 10, Armin Newerla was arrested for the first time. On August 14, a bomb exploded in the Stuttgart office that Müller and Newerla shared, destroying most of it. Their office had been repeatedly described in the press as a RAF "recruitment center." After this, we could get no news from the prisoners on Stammheim's seventh floor. We didn't know how they were doing, and we didn't know if we should continue the strike. The propaganda machine was running at full throttle against us, and the struggle was very hard for each of us alone in our cells.

Just as in 1974, I once again lost my courage and my strength. It became clear to me, and to all the others, that we were not going to be able to win back our previous conditions with this strike. Once I realized that, I found it more and more difficult to keep on going while waiting for us to reach a joint decision. The same thing happened in this strike as had happened three years earlier—at a critical point in the struggle, my personal decision entered into conflict with the collective decision. I ended my strike a few days before the others, as did Ilse. The rest of the prisoners broke off their strike on September 2. It was clear that continuing the strike would only have led to people dying, without any change in prison conditions.

Having resumed eating before a hunger strike had been collectively ended for a second time, I keenly felt the need to reexamine and question my capabilities and ideas. Given the situation and what I had been through, I had to distance myself from the other prisoners, from the group, to have the space I needed to find my own path. I applied to be transferred to a regular prison in Frankfurt. In 1975, when I was in bad shape after the hunger strike, and then once again in 1976, the prison administration had offered to transfer me to the Frankfurt prison, with the idea of "reuniting the family," as my parents lived in Bonn, and Frankfurt was the nearest women's prison. At that time, it had been completely out of the question for me, but now I saw it as an opportunity. The other RAF prisoners once again viewed my decision as a political betrayal. Inga tried to talk to me about it, but I didn't want to argue anymore.

There wasn't any time left for talk anyway—three days after the end of the strike, on September 5, the Siegfried Hausner Commando kidnapped the president of the Federal Association of German Employers, Hanns Martin Schleyer. In the process, the guerrillas shot and killed three policemen and Schleyer's chauffeur. In exchange for Schleyer's release, the unit demanded the release of eleven prisoners from the RAF.

Federal Chancellor Helmut Schmidt reacted to this action by putting together a "small Crisis Management Team," which assumed decision-making power. A state of emergency existed; it was war. One and a half years later, Schmidt made the following statement: "I wish to thank the German jurists for not examining all of that under constitutional law." For the first time in the history of the Federal Republic of Germany, a gag order was imposed on the press, which were only allowed to print official statements. Every possible form of public oversight was cut off.

At the same time, an unprecedented witch hunt targeted everyone on the left. The aim of those in power, who had declared a state of emergency, was to force people to distance themselves from the guerrilla. Many yielded to the pressure. The Crisis Management Team and the press discussed bringing back the death penalty and threatened to start shooting political prisoners to force Schleyer's release.

All contact with the outside and on the inside was cut off for us prisoners. With no legal basis, a Contact Ban was imposed on all of the roughly one hundred people imprisoned in connection with Paragraph 129. This applied to the prisoners from other guerrilla groups just as much as it did to those from the RAF. Prisoners who had distanced themselves from their groups were subject to the same conditions as those who continued to support the armed struggle. The Contact Ban meant that we were no longer allowed yard time. They took away our radios, withheld newspapers and letters, and denied us visits, including with our lawyers. Total isolation. Nothing from the outside world could get through to us, and nobody on the outside heard anything from us. This created space for the state to do whatever it wanted.

It was BKA chief Horst Herold's hour of glory. With support from the government and the state judicial authorities, and over the objections of federal judges and federal public prosecutors, he imposed a ban on visits from defense lawyers. This created a grotesque situation, whereby lawyers who had been given explicit consent by a judge and who were backed by the Office of the Federal Prosecutor would be waiting for their clients in the visiting rooms, while the prison administration refused to bring the prisoners to them. The BKA got its way by referring to the "state of emergency." Parliament followed suit: within three days, the Contact Ban law was rushed through, legalizing what would be the longest Contact Ban ever implemented. The claim that the RAF prisoners were leading and organizing political operations from their cells was used to justify this law. Six months later, Minister of Justice Vogel, when asked on Italian television if the Schleyer kidnapping had been planned and controlled from within the prison cells, answered: "No. We didn't even think so at the time, and there was nothing to indicate that that could have been the case." The Crisis Management Team turned us prisoners into hostages of the state, just like in a military dictatorship.

I was treated the same as all of the other political prisoners. Almost all of my personal belongings were taken from me—my notes, most of my books, writing materials, clothes, radio, and files. I was allowed to keep a few books and was given some lined sheets of prison paper that had been counted, a prison pen, prison overalls, and prison underwear. There was no music anymore. Although there was almost nothing left in my cell, it was still searched every day, both during my solitary yard time and when I was in my cell. At least once a week, I was taken to an empty cell, where I had to strip naked in front of two female guards and change my clothes. The few possessions I had were packed in a shoe box, and then I was moved to a new empty cell. After four or five days, the same procedure was repeated. On several occasions, a whole squad of BKA officers turned up to search and examine everything.

For hours on end, I would stand on my chair at the window and look out through the bars at the prison walls. Sometimes I fantasized about being a very normal woman with a very normal profession. I wanted to get away from this never-ending pressure. I had now been in prison for almost five years, with one shitty year on the outside in between sentences. The confrontation, both on the inside and on the outside, had been steadily worsening, and I was less and less able to bear it. I wanted the eleven prisoners to be released, but I had become a spectator. And, once again, it was the state apparatus that had brought me to this point. Why had a Contact Ban been imposed on me? I was a hostage of the state. For them, it was never about people. They only cared about their own power—it was all about collaboration, revenge, or steamrolling people. The pressure was enormous. It was only rarely that one of the other prisoners dared to shout the news from the radio to us, and the guards immediately clamped down hard on such attempts. It was a situation where anything could happen, and my nerves were at their breaking point.

On September 30, attorney Arndt Müller was arrested. The arrest warrant was issued on the grounds that he had worked in the same office as attorney Klaus Croissant, who was arrested at the same time in Paris, and Armin Newerla, who had already been arrested on August 30, and that sympathizers who had now gone underground had frequented their office.

On October 13, a Palestinian commando unit hijacked a German passenger plane on its way from Majorca to West Germany, flying it to South Yemen, and then to Mogadishu, the capital city of Somalia. The guerrillas demanded the release of the eleven prisoners in the FRG, as well as Palestinian prisoners in Turkey and Israel.

Following the intervention of US president Jimmy Carter, in the early morning hours of October 18, and with the help of British counterinsurgency experts, a German special "anti-terrorist" unit, the Border Protection Group 9 (Grenzschutzgruppe 9, GSG-9), stormed the plane and killed the entire Palestinian commando unit with the exception of Souhaila Andrawes, who survived but was seriously injured.

A few hours later, Andreas Baader and Jan-Carl Raspe were found dead in their cells from gunshot wounds, Gudrun Ensslin was found hanged, and Irmgard Möller was found seriously injured by four stab wounds from a blunt prison knife. The propaganda machine delivered its verdict immediately: suicide. The prisoners had been desperate and, in the end, had gotten what they deserved.

I heard about it the next morning, when the prison director opened the door to my cell, accompanied by a BKA officer. "The prisoners Baader, Ensslin, Raspe, and Möller have committed suicide in Stammheim. The BKA has, therefore, ordered that all prisoners currently subject to the Contact Ban be placed under special observation to prevent further suicides." The flap in my cell door, through which they could observe me around the clock, was opened once again.

I got up on the chair at the barred window and looked out at the prison walls. There was nothing in me but a deep and infinite sadness. Things had gone on too long to end well. But suicide? No, certainly not that. The government had created all the conditions it needed to be able to act. The small Crisis Management Team had made use of the ample means at its disposal. Now the pressure was being intensified on those who weren't dead by keeping us under constant observation. They hoped that one of us would commit suicide, unable to stand it any longer.

Was this the end of trying to implement the urban guerrilla strategy in the Federal Republic of Germany? What would happen now? I had already distanced myself and had decided to go my own way. The developments of the past weeks did nothing to change that. However, they had once again reaffirmed my decision to have nothing to do with the state apparatus. I wouldn't make peace with the state, even if I was no longer able to fight. I also had my doubts about the direction in which the RAF was heading. The guerrilla had sought out an extreme confrontation that I could no longer go along with.

When Schleyer was found dead in the trunk of a car on October 19, I was not surprised. What other option was there given the circumstances? Could they really have released him after the plane was stormed in Mogadishu and after the deaths of the RAF members in Stammheim? Would that not have made the state's victory absolute? What kind of person had Schleyer been? Did his history no longer exist, his responsibility in perpetuating policies that never counted the countless dead? Yet his death didn't make any sense either.

On November 12, RAF prisoner Ingrid Schubert was found dead in her cell in Stadelheim prison, in Bavaria. She had been transferred there in August, when the Stammheim group, of which she had been a member, was broken up, and had been held in extreme isolation until her unexplained death. Had they finally managed to drive her to suicide? I had no answers.

With Schleyer dead, the Contact Ban was formally lifted, but we prisoners were still kept in strict isolation. At the end of November, we went on a short hunger strike, which I participated in. I saw no other way of protesting against the de facto ongoing Contact Ban. Like the others, I had to get out of there, even if I ultimately wanted to go somewhere else. This hunger strike caused days of cramps and unbearable headaches for me, and these have stayed with me to this very day whenever I get hungry or tired.

As previously mentioned, the lawyers Arndt Müller and Armin Newerla had been arrested before the Stammheim deaths. They were later charged with having smuggled the weapons with which the prisoners were said to have killed themselves into the high security wing in Stammheim and were sentenced to four years and eight months and three years and six months in prison respectively.

In early 1978, I was transferred to Frankfurt-Preungesheim, with regular prison conditions.

A Normal Prison

In Preungesheim, I suddenly found myself in a place where my cell door was left open. Next to me and on the three floors above me, other prisoners laughed, talked to one another or ranted, or eyed me, the newcomer, with curiosity. I had to muster all my courage to leave my cell and expose myself to their looks and questions. After years of isolation and the Contact Ban, being surrounded by so many people I didn't know scared me and made me shy. With a great deal of effort and the help of the other women, I learned how to open up to people again, to laugh, to stop sounding like a telegram when I spoke, and to express myself in a way that others could understand.

I also started working. In a large room with simple machines, thirty women glued together plastic bags and folded cardboard boxes. The humdrum, monotonous gluing of plastic bags was a relief for me in those first weeks. After years alone in my cell, I was able to move around in a large space. There were always conversations going on within the three-woman work units and between the different groups. Unaccustomed to the work and to being around other people, I was exhausted by the time evening came. But, gradually, I got to know the world of the women in prison, their stories, their strategies for survival. It was a special world, with its own language and its own code of conduct.

I quickly made friends with a few prisoners who had been convicted for heroin-related crimes. Most of them were not politically conscious, but we understood each other in our rejection of the values of "normal" society. They had mostly started using heroin out of desperation, because they couldn't find a path in life and didn't want to live as they were expected to. They came from different family backgrounds, their fathers included blue-collar workers and salaried employees; many had left school without any qualifications, while others had finished an apprenticeship of some kind. No matter what the differences between them, they were all really sharp when they weren't using H. When they were clean, they had no trouble identifying oppression and exploitation, and they rebelled against it. They accepted me as one of them and wanted to know what I thought of the articles they wrote in the prison newspaper.

Christine was a qualified medical assistant; small and thin, she liked to wear bright clothes that got her noticed and took great care applying her make-up. In this way, she was different from Ingrid and the other ex-junkies, who generally didn't care what they looked like. Nonetheless, while she liked taking care of her appearance, it was never so important to her that she wouldn't be able to give it up if necessary. She was generous, and it made her happy when she could share a chocolate bar or a homemade cake from the birthday package her mother had sent her with Ingrid and me.

Ingrid didn't get parcels from anyone. She had been shooting up since she was thirteen, just like her sister who lied on another floor in Preungesheim with acute cirrhosis of the liver. She didn't have any school qualifications and yet to her own surprise, she now discovered that she loved searching through newspapers and books with us to find some piece of information, reading stories, or even writing articles for the prison newspaper.

With Ingrid and Christine, I rediscovered forgotten needs: eating something delicious or the smell of perfumed soap; cream for my skin, which was always dry and cracked easily; listening to music together.

One day, when I had been at Preungesheim for about six weeks, we were sitting in the common room and I noticed one of the women watching me silently. She was almost as big as I was, young, and from the "ghetto," which is what she called the postwar temporary housing estate where she had grown up. Through her relationships with GIs stationed at the military camp near where she lived, she had started doing drugs and had become an addict. After some time, she started speaking to me. "I didn't know who you were, but I liked you from the very beginning, and I've liked everything I've seen about you since. About half an hour ago, somebody told me why you're in prison, that you're one of the terrorists." She had a shocked expression on her face. "That's when I suddenly realized what was going on in my head. Before getting to know you, I always wanted people like you to be hanged. I hated you and thought you were the worst and the evilest of murderers. I only knew about you all from *Bild* and television. I didn't actually know any of you. To me, you were pigs, the worst kind of criminals. Now, I feel sick when I think that I wanted to have you hanged, that I really hated you all. It makes me want to cry."

For the first time in over five years, I got to "go to the movies," as social workers would occasionally pick out a film for us. A screen was hung on the wall of the largest room, which also served for church services on Sundays. One day, we sat pressed closely together on rows of chairs; Ingrid and Christine were next to me. The film began, *State of Siege* by Costa-Gavras. The images captivated me and kept me entranced. It was a film about the Tupamaros in Uruguay, the activities of the urban guerrilla movement there, and military and police repression, built around the kidnapping of CIA agent Daniel Mitrione and his captivity in a "people's prison." I couldn't believe I was able to see a film like that in prison. It stirred deeply buried memories, and I realized that the world outside, especially the time before my arrest, hardly existed in my conscious mind anymore. Nor did that feeling of taking the bull by the horns and forcing it to its knees, which I also had previously felt.

Christine had already seen the film and had also taken part in left-wing discussions in the mid-1970s not far from where she lived. She had been involved in the squatters' movement before discovering heroin. She began to think about those times and shared some of her stories with us.

Then I fell in love. After years of isolation, I had forgotten what it was like to fall in love. It took me completely by surprise, dragging me into a whirlwind of emotions.

Karin was older than me, always on the go, enigmatic, full of stories. She had been a lesbian all her life, coming from a world that was previously unknown to me, the world of women who felt discriminated against in society and had created their own subculture separate from men.

In prison, many women have sexual relationships with other women. The loneliness and the loss of all other relationships create pressure, and women in prison search for the only alternative at hand—a relationship with a fellow prisoner. A strange set of double standards emerges, a life in two worlds that exist parallel to one another. The women have the same ideas and moral standards as the outside world, completely rejecting lesbian relationships and despising prisoners who actually are lesbians, that is, who love other women even when on the outside. At the same time, they have sexual relations with other prisoners, which they do not see as lesbian relationships, but as substitutes for relationships with men. The substitute relationships are kept secret and, while everyone knows what is going on, nobody talks about it.

I only really became aware of these double standards as my feelings for Karin grew stronger. I already knew what it was like to be discriminated against because of my political convictions. I now became aware of the threat of this other form of discrimination and realized that society's hostility toward a way of being cuts much deeper, calling into

question your existence and your very understanding of
yourself as a human being. I had to consciously fight to not
give in to my fear, to not give in when faced with contempt,
but to openly stick by my feelings. Meanwhile, Karin told
me about her life, about how harsh society's discrimination
against gays and lesbians had been in the 1960s and what
she had done to survive. Her response to this hatred was to
reject any and all heterosexual relationships, and she had
grown angry at all men. This was something I could relate
to, and the combination of feeling threatened in prison and
of my feelings for Karin led me to decide that as an act of solidarity with all lesbian women I would not have any further
relationships with men. To do otherwise would have felt like
a betrayal.

Karin had cancer. She had been operated on a year earlier,
but the tumor in her uterus could not be completely removed,
and she had been supposed to have another operation
within six months. By that point, however, she was already
in prison. Now the pain had started again, and the fear she
had suppressed returned in the form of panic. She had been
sentenced to six months for tax fraud and had already served
more than half of it. The normal legal avenues for having a
sentence suspended took forever and would mean, first of
all, filing an application with the judge in Munich, where
Karin had been sentenced, waiting for a response from the
Public Prosecutor, then for a decision by the Court for the
Execution of Prison Sentences. Karin no longer left her cell;
she had stopped eating, and she cried all the time.

The prison administration could have acted, suspended
the sentence, and taken Karin to a hospital, because her life
was in danger, but they did nothing. I discussed what we
could do with Christine, Ingrid, and a small group of prisoners. We circulated a petition demanding immediate parole,
then brought it to the prison director, warning her, "If Karin
doesn't get out in the next few days, we will cause trouble in

the prison!" I knew that the consequences for making a threat like this could be transfer to another prison and renewed isolation. This seemed unimportant, however, in view of the possibility of rescuing Karin from certain death from cancer. The next day, she was taken to a hospital, operated on, and told she didn't have to return to prison. She visited me regularly right up until my release; the cancer never came back, and I remained in regular prison in Preungesheim.

In April 1978, RAF prisoner Verena Becker was transferred to Preungesheim. Since the official end of the Contact Ban, the conditions for most of the political prisoners had remained unchanged, which meant that they were basically the same as when the Contact Ban had been in force. So the RAF prisoners had begun a new hunger strike, which ended with the prison authorities reintroducing their previous practice of differentiated prison conditions. Some prisoners remained in total isolation, while others were brought together in very small groups. Verena was transferred to Frankfurt into normal prison.

To make sure that we had as little contact as possible, I was given painters' overalls, a brush, and paint, and assigned to paint cells, while Verena was sent to glue plastic bags. Her cell was in the same wing as mine, one floor above me. As there weren't any walls between the floors, but only waist-high grate balustrades and lattice doors to the mostly open stairs, there wasn't much to get in the way of our communicating. Besides, we had our daily yard time together. But Verena didn't want to have anything to do with me. She made it clear to the other prisoners that there was a distance and a difference between us. For Verena, as for the other remaining prisoners from the RAF, I was someone who had changed politically, who didn't want to fight anymore, someone who could no longer be trusted or relied upon.

I knew what the others thought of me but had still been happy when I heard Verena was being transferred to

Preungesheim, and her reaction hurt me. However, I gritted my teeth and told myself maybe it was better this way, because now I wouldn't have to struggle with the temptation to do something out of solidarity that wasn't consistent with my own view of things, because she expected it of me or simply to avoid conflict. Verena's rejection made things difficult, but that's exactly what I had been looking for when I applied to a regular prison—a chance to make decisions based only on my own thinking and inclination, and I had made real progress in that regard.

It became clear that in certain situations we thought the same, responded to certain problems the same way, and that we got on well with the same prisoners. It also became clear that my decision to separate from the group didn't mean that I had chosen the most comfortable path or one without struggle, or that I was looking to fit in; it simply meant that to deal with my own self-doubt I had to work on myself.

During all the years I was in prison, my mother had never stopped writing to me. At some point, this convinced me that she loved me in her own way, and that she had never given up on me. My father, on the other hand, had never made a single attempt. He was incapable of taking the smallest step in my direction, although he also loved me in his way. In Preungesheim, no longer subject to the intense pressure of isolation, I was in a position where I felt I could accept visits from my family again. Previously, such visits had taken place in a special cell, where the visitor sat at one end of a long table, while an officer from the BKA sat at the other end and wrote everything down, and at least one guard skulked behind me. Now, like all the other prisoners, I had access to the large visiting room, filled with many prisoners and their friends and family, sitting and talking at small tables and eating things the people from the outside had brought with them. The room was full of noise, and a single guard stood in the doorway watching us all. It was finally possible to have a real conversation.

We had all learned our lesson. After all of the times I had rebuffed their attempts to make contact, my parents now understood that they couldn't interfere in my decisions, and they no longer tried to. My mother even called up the newspapers to complain when the term isolation torture was printed in scare quotes, telling them it truly was torture by isolation. When I told her that I was in love with a woman, she wrote to me that she understood what I was going through, because the same had happened to her once, but she had decided to marry my father and have a family instead. I really respected her openness in these letters, because I knew how much something like that was despised in her milieu. She was the only family member with whom I was able to rebuild a close relationship, and she died one year after my release from prison.

In the meantime, my brother Dieter had joined an Indian sect. When the student movement came to an end, various religious movements from Asia had become popular in Europe and North America. Many people flocked to these sects; people looking for a new direction, including very young people who had no desire to fit into the capitalist world of competition and consumption. They were attracted by the idea of life in paradise that was preached by the leaders, as well as by a chance to escape from the unbearable pressure of a highly competitive society. Most of these sects had an authoritarian-patriarchal structure, and the main interest of the "gurus" was to financially exploit their followers. By the time I was released, Dieter was half a million marks (over a quarter million dollars) in debt, money that he had donated to the sect. The first year, he did up to eight hours of transcendental meditation a day. This exhausted him to such an extent that my parents didn't even recognize him on the street. His face had changed completely. Over time, he became a brutal person, greedy for money, and I broke off all contact with him. He remained in the sect until he died, ten years later, when he drove his car into a tree.

The longer I spent in normal prison, the more I regained my self-awareness, which also meant I became increasingly aware of the effects normal prison was having on me. All of my time was spent dealing with the day-to-day problems of other prisoners; someone or another was always coming to me with her problems, or somewhere, someone was flipping out because she couldn't stand things anymore, and so we had to help her get back on her feet. There were arguments and confrontations with the guards and the prison administration. I hardly had the time to read the newspaper. Studying a weighty book had become totally impossible.

Christine and Ingrid, the prisoners I hung around with the most, were released. Shortly after that, they both went back to the needle. New prisoners arrived, and things were in a constant state of flux.

What would it be like when I got out? My sentence was due to end in autumn 1979. Would they really let me out? How could I be sure that they wouldn't initiate new proceedings against me like they had with Irmgard Möller and Bernhard Braun? At the end of her sentence, Irmgard had been transferred to Stammheim, and the new charges that were filed against her resulted in a life sentence. I was now going my own particular way, but that didn't mean I was at all safe from the same kind of arbitrary cruelty. Bernhard, for example, had distanced himself from the group long before they brought him up on new charges on the day of his release. What I had experienced in Lübeck had taught me that when it came to State Security, I had to be on my guard and always prepared for the worst.

If they really did release me—what would I do then?

I tried to imagine my life on the outside. I didn't want to distance myself or denounce anyone, but I also no longer

wanted to take part in the armed struggle. However, I also
wasn't prepared to accept things the way they were. After
what I had experienced in prison since 1971, I saw myself in
a kind of trap that offered me only two options: on the one
hand, to become numb to everything or to denounce people,
both of which amounted to the same thing for me, or, on the
other hand, to attack the state head on, which meant continuing to work with the guerrilla. Neither option appealed
to me.

I spoke with Verena about my fears and thoughts, as well
as with Monika, the social worker who was in charge of my
file. At first, I hadn't trusted her—I felt certain that there was
no way a social worker in prison could be okay. However,
watching her work with the other prisoners in our section I
had learned to respect her. She had supported our demand
to have Karin released and had also taken our side in other
conflicts with the prison administration. She was younger
than me and likable. She suggested that I file an application
for early release, as I had served two-thirds of my sentence.
This was the usual practice for other prisoners, but not for
those of us from the RAF. We had always rejected this option,
because its success depended on a favorable social prognosis,
which in our case meant renunciation. Should I get into that?
What could I say without denouncing my comrades? And
what did I even want to do afterward?

I decided I did not want to stay in Germany; I wanted
to go to Africa, to Guinea-Bissau, Mozambique, or Angola.
However, even after liberation from Portuguese colonial rule,
the situation there had not improved. After five hundred
years of plundering, the Portuguese had left behind countries that were completely lacking in infrastructure. There
were a few military barracks and military airports but no
schools, no universities, no roads, no jobs, no doctors. Big
corporations and the countries' governments remained as
interested as ever in raw materials. Supported by the US and

South Africa, armed groups were fighting against the governments of Mozambique and Angola. The tribal differences that had been exploited by the Portuguese were still being stirred up. The war had not stopped and neither had hunger, misery, and despair. I couldn't go there.

Monika brought me several pamphlets about projects in Third World countries, and she knew of a development project in Tanzania. However, to work there, I would have to be able to do something practical, otherwise what was the point? I decided to learn carpentry and study architecture. Monika got in touch with a professor at Frankfurt University who specialized in architecture in tropical Third World countries, and he came to see me in prison.

Finally, I filed the standard application for early release after serving two-thirds of my sentence. At my hearing before the Court for the Execution of Prison Sentences at the end of Autumn 1978, I declared that I personally would no longer engage in armed struggle, but I refused to make any political statement whatsoever concerning the politics of the guerrilla.

We got reinforcements in November: Helga, Rosi, Ingrid, and Simone, together with others, had occupied the Frankfurt offices of the Deutsche Presse-Agentur (dpa) news agency to draw attention to the life-threatening situations of Werner Hoppe and Karl-Heinz Dellwo. After seven years in isolation, Werner, with whom I had had such an intense correspondence during my initial period in prison, weighed only 44kg and was no longer able to keep food down. He lay there in hospital in Hamburg; his doctors said he was medically unfit to remain in prison, yet they refused to release him. Despite the many attempts by his lawyers and his family to publicize his situation, the press remained silent. Since Schleyer's death, the situation of the political prisoners and their prison conditions had been completely hushed up. Karl-Heinz, a member of the commando that had occupied the embassy in Stockholm, had been on hunger and thirst strike for six weeks to protest against his treatment and the isolation conditions.

These four women were brought to the remand prisoners' wing and remained isolated there. However, they showered together with the other prisoners and went to the canteen with them, so Verena and I could see them. There were now six of us political prisoners mixed in with the regular prisoners. Intense discussions were happening all over the prison; the oppressive stillness born of powerlessness was gone. The response was increased control and repression. Even though not technically allowed, it hadn't been a problem previously to go from one section to another—now doors with bars on them were installed between different areas. The prison newspaper starting having problems, with articles being censored or banned outright. The prison administration wanted to be able to dictate what was printed in it, something they had lost control over. Finally, the newspaper was closed down. We organized discussions and meetings to vote in a prison council, which the prison regulations permitted, but which until then had always been appointed by the administration.

There was a new prison director, Kuhlenkampf, a smart young guy direct from the Ministry.

My application for early release, which had been accepted by the Court for the Execution of Prison Sentences, was rejected by the Higher Regional Court. The reason? No evidence of active remorse.

Things really heated up in the women's prison when Günter Sonnenberg went on hunger strike to protest against his separation from two other political prisoners and against his transfer from Stammheim to Bruchsal. The remaining RAF prisoners joined this strike. At the time of his arrest, in May 1977, Günter had been shot in the head and seriously injured and had suffered from amnesia ever since. He could no longer read or write and could hardly talk. He had been medically unfit for prison from the start, but they still placed him in total isolation. With amazing strength of will, he began to recover his memory. After a year, he was allowed to exercise in the yard with two RAF prisoners, but the transfer meant that this would no longer be possible.

Günter had been arrested along with Verena, and she was able to tell us more about him. Many of the women in prison were disgusted at how the courts and State Security were persecuting Günter, placing him in isolation despite his head injury. We discussed whether or not we wanted to join in the hunger strike. There were several regular prisoners who would have loved to start right away. However, Verena and the women who had occupied the dpa offices first wanted to talk about the consequences of a hunger strike for everyone involved. At the end of February 1979, the four "dpa women" joined the strike. When they were isolated as a result, we organized a petition. Sixty prisoners protested against the four women being locked down, and some women, Verena and I among them, went on hunger strike. The strike escalated in March, with a short thirst strike, and more prisoners joined us. At that point, the Ministry of Justice agreed to transfer Günter back to Stammheim to be with the other two RAF prisoners.

The prison administration responded with threats: stricter controls, canceling prison leave and other "privileges," locking prisoners in their cells, yard time alone. This pressure polarized the prisoners: some got scared and sided with the administration, trying to foment hatred against us, because we "agitated" among the other prisoners and "used them for our own agenda." The rest of the women fought alongside us for our rights and our dignity, and a spirit of solidarity, closeness, and strength developed among us, something that was completely new for many of them. They discovered that it can be fun to struggle side by side.

One Wednesday in early April, Helga, Rosi, Ingrid, and Simone were on their way back from the trial for the dpa occupation, when they were attacked by a bunch of guards. Rosi was beaten so badly that the hyoid bone in her neck was broken. This attack did not take place in the cellblock, but we found out about it immediately, and we saw that they were rushing to clear out the wing above the administration, with the obvious aim of isolating the four women there. It was early afternoon, and we gathered at the platform, a small "square" at the spot where the four wings of the building met below the guards' control center. What could we do to protest against the use of physical violence and the transfer of the four women to isolation? A small group of prisoners, Verena and I among them, remained on the platform to inform all of the women. Everyone coming from work, from trial, or from a visit had to go by the platform, so our group gradually grew bigger. The small metal food trolleys rolled through the sections, and the guards called out, "Grub's up! Anybody not in their cell won't be getting any food!" We didn't care, we stayed on the platform. The head guard ordered the doors to the sections closed. This meant we couldn't get in, and the prisoners in their sections couldn't get to us.

The security inspector appeared. "If you do not go to your cells immediately," he threatened, "we will initiate proceedings against you for agitation and mutiny. Then not only can you forget early release, you will be facing more time! I demand that you get down from the platform immediately!" He stood there, confident that we would give in to his intimidation. However, only a few women decided to go back to their cells, while the rest of us, maybe fifteen or twenty prisoners, pulled together. It was now evening, and they had locked in all of the women early. Some of them banged against their doors in solidarity, and then all of a sudden we heard one of them shout, "The pigs! The pigs are outside!"

The prison administration had called in the heavies. At that very moment, the doors to the administrative section and to the yard opened, and the guards were pushing their way through. Many of the prisoners now started banging against their doors, and the whole prison reverberated with the noise. We asked if we could talk among ourselves, and we decided to go back to our cells and yield to the guards' superior numbers. We were chaperoned back to our cells, but for hours after, we hammered against the wooden doors with such fury that the guards ran up and down the corridors, anxious and afraid we might beat the doors down, and, in fact, one door did break. It was pandemonium.

In the end, we managed to prevent the four women from being transferred to the vacated wing.

Since I had arrived at Preungesheim prison, I had repeatedly witnessed how a few individual prisoners made it possible to smuggle drugs inside despite the thousands of controls. However, after we started getting organized and there was solidarity between us women, drugs suddenly became ubiquitous, and nobody knew where they were coming from. A lot of the women we were friends with were former junkies. Now that they were being offered heroin so easily, many of them couldn't resist, and this part of our solidarity broke away. The prisoners who began to shoot up fell back into their old patterns of isolation, selfishness, suspicion, and denunciation. It was terrible to see how people changed from one day to the next because of the drugs. We were, however, almost completely powerless against it. Under these difficult conditions, drugs were stronger than we were.

One month after our collective stand for the four comrades, I was released. Our appeal against the Higher Regional Court's objection had been successful, and I got out on parole a few months before the end of my sentence. It was May 11, 1979.

I moved in with my friend Karin. It very quickly became clear that I didn't need to go to Africa, and that I had a number of options.

I was thirty-one years old, and, since 1971, I had spent seventy-five months in various prisons for forging passports and possessing weapons that had never been used, but, first and foremost, for supporting and being a member of the RAF.

And here I was starting once again, "from the beginning."

Postscript (2007)

When I was released from prison in 1979, I joined some other people and began to organize solidarity for the political prisoners. Visits with the prisoners were largely forbidden, and there was hardly any public debate about prison conditions.

Together with other women, I set up an anti-imperialist women's group and, in the years that followed, played an active role in various discussions and groups.

In August 1985, I left the country, because they were threatening to arrest me for a third time—the use of preventive detention had already been announced on television. I applied for and was granted political asylum in Cuba.

There, I thought about writing down my story.

In prison, we had already discussed the fact that there would have to be memoirs about our history one day, not only documentary reports with political statements or more or less "objective" analyses of social conflicts and the overall context. But who would write them? The prisoners were unable to, as the isolation conditions made this impossible. In addition, our cells were constantly being raided and all of our documents stolen.

From 1979 to 1985, I noticed that many of the young people who were becoming political, especially in the anti-NATO movement in 1980, knew nothing about the 1970s, nothing about the student movement, and nothing about our experiences in prison and the intensity of our conflict with the state. I was always being asked about it, and they wanted me to tell them what it had been like.

In Cuba, I started to think that I should write down at least part of the RAF's history. Initially, I found it difficult to write. I was just getting used to life in Cuba and was learning Spanish. In 1988, my twins were born, and all of my energy went into looking after them.

In 1991, I finally began. It was a hard battle for my memories. Over the past fifteen to twenty years, I had hardly spoken about what had happened. I hadn't spoken about it in Germany, because we talked about the state's objectives, not what we had been subjected to. I hadn't spoken about it in Cuba, because the Cuban government had made not talking about it a condition for my being granted asylum. I was also not supposed to talk about the fact that I had been granted asylum. And the Cubans who I trusted could not imagine what it meant in Europe, where the people had everything, to engage in revolutionary struggle and to have been in prison as a result. It took me over six months to produce one hundred pages.

When I shared my text with a few German friends, they reacted with disbelief. "It can't have been like that!" they said. They also said, "Politically, it's the wrong time" or "You can't write it like that." As I myself was unsure, I locked the manuscript away in a drawer at the bottom of a cupboard.

I thought I could try to live in Germany again and wanted to return there with my family in 1992. However, when I heard that people from the Office for the Protection of the Constitution were waiting at the Berlin airport on the day of my planned arrival, as well as the news of attacks on refugees in Rostock and the continued mistreatment of the prisoners, I thought better of it. Instead, we moved to Uruguay in 1993.

In Uruguay, I began discussing my project with Tupamaros who had been in prison and made another attempt to talk to comrades in Germany about our history, but I received no reply. I thought about it for a while, and then sat down again with the old manuscript.

While I was writing, I was unsure if young people today

would understand me. My German came from 1985; both my language and my way of thinking were from back then. Prior to 2000, the year after this book was first published, I hadn't been back to Europe at all. One interview that I read in *taz* newspaper made me stop and think. In the article, four young women were asked their opinion of Ulrike Meinhof and the RAF. One of them answered, "These RAF women were pretty strange. On the one hand, they reckoned they were really emancipated and, on the other hand, they were so dependent on men that they couldn't free Andreas Baader with a group of women but needed the help of a man." Her criticism was based on the fact that the women who freed Andreas in 1970 decided at the last minute to bring a man into the commando unit, because they feared that the men guarding Andreas wouldn't take them seriously, and that they would, as a result, be forced to shoot.

Then, in 2000, I met some young people on my first journey back to Germany who maybe spoke another language, but who were nevertheless curious and weren't put off by the fact that we had different ways of talking about things. Once again, I was given a chance to learn.

On that trip, I encountered an old phenomenon: I was besieged by the press. The very same journalists who wanted me to declare that I was against violence wrote pieces justifying the Gulf War (although Germany had no soldiers on the battlefield) and the attack on Yugoslavia (the first time since 1945 that German soldiers were deployed). They argued that these wars were necessary. In the Germany of 2001, Foreign Minister Joschka Fischer was expected to show remorse and resign when it was revealed that he had eaten breakfast with me thirty years earlier. At the same time, he was congratulated for giving the order to carry out a war of aggression against Yugoslavia that resulted in the deaths of thousands of civilians. Enormous pressure is exerted on anyone who had once set their hopes on revolution, all to validate that special German dogma that the state is always in the right. Many succumbed and still succumb to this day. All that remains is the idea that each person should take care of number one, with the result that we will be paying for the air we breathe if the transnational pharmaceutical companies continue to get their way.

In late 2002, my book was released in Spanish. The reaction to its publication in Montevideo showed me that I had written it primarily for my Uruguayan friends. I lived with them, and they were in my thoughts when I was searching for the right words to use. Nearly all of them had spent many years in prison, many had lived in exile, and almost all of them had children who were the same age as my twins. The female ex-prisoners wanted a collective work about their history with a collective result. Conflicts within the group were not discussed, not even more than ten years after their release from prison. My work found a context that gave me strength and self-confidence. In Germany, there were only a few of us; in Uruguay, more than a thousand. Germany had the isolation conditions, in Uruguay there were large groups of women held in a single prison camp, while the men were all placed in isolation in one large prison. In Germany, the ex-prisoners lived in different cities and in different realities after their release. In Uruguay, they kept in touch personally even after their release, and they also experienced similar realities—yet despite all this, the questions, problems, thoughts, and practices were very similar at their core, both here and there. Realizing this helped me write.

When my Uruguayan friends read my book, they were astonished that there could be so many similarities across the continents without there having been any personal contact. Depoliticization and treating an interest in politics as a psychiatric issue is the usual practice in Germany, where, to portray us as a handful of lunatics, they try to eliminate any awareness of any context beyond the country's borders.

In 2003, I made the difficult decision to return to Germany. The banking system in Uruguay had collapsed, and the Dresdner Bank, Credit Suisse, and Chase Manhattan in Montevideo went bankrupt. It was an amazing thing to watch. The government pumped Uruguayan state finances into the holes through which huge amounts of money had been sucked out of Uruguay and into the metropoles. All that was left was the ruins of a country. Like many other people, I no longer knew how to feed my children. In 2002, seventy thousand Uruguayans emigrated, out of a total population of three million. The exodus continues and, as always, it is the most highly qualified who leave and are granted access to the rich countries.

From the beginning, it was clear to me that I could only write about the time up to my second release from prison. Prior to 1979, I was alone most of the time, especially in prison, only ever momentarily taking part in any group, and many of those I worked with are no longer alive. After 1979, I was in various groups in which those involved would engage in intense discussions, and I didn't think I should reconstruct this process on my own.

Anyone who expected my book to document and judge the guerrilla's theoretical foundations must be disappointed. That is neither my story nor my aim. I joined the RAF without having spent years studying the theory of revolution, yet I did not take this path by chance. There was and still is a continuous thread running through my life that started back then—to always search for new ways to fight against injustice and not to shy away from the personal consequences. In this overintellectualized Germany, many on the left do not want to accept something that is celebrated by the people of the so-called Third World: that a person can take up the struggle without having analyzed the world theoretically beforehand. Struggling in this way does not mean they are blind; in fact, this struggle emerges from a political situation and a lived political conviction. There was not even one year between my first step toward a conscious search for political practice (Release) and my arrest in 1971. I wasn't going to reread political analyses from the 1960s and 1970s (as I did during my time in prison) in order to reconstruct the theoretical background for this book. That would have meant another eight years before this book was published, and, besides, those were theories that I was hardly familiar with at the time. After a great many doubts about myself, I came to the conclusion that it still made sense to write an account of what I had experienced.

I have not written my story to place it in a drawer and be finished with it, as if the story is at an end and the same questions and injustices no longer exist.

To get a more accurate picture, there have to be many accounts. I think we should be as open as possible about our experiences, otherwise the discussion about the RAF will remain stuck somewhere between mythology and psychological warfare. I am certainly not talking about the admissions of remorse and guilt that are loudly demanded by those who unabashedly support the wars for oil and other natural resources and strive for ideological supremacy while millions of people die. Today, those who are dying are mainly dying in Africa, Iraq, and Afghanistan, and they are dying in the thousands—while those in power wash their hands, as if innocent.

Afterword
by Osvaldo Bayer (2001)

Margrit Schiller's book took me back to the 1960s and 1970s and to the questions for which there were no answers. Not about Germany, but about my country: Argentina. The same problem in two completely different scenarios. The circumstances were different, but the questions were the same and continue to be the same—despite one being in the First World and the other in the Third World.

But what was strange was that Margrit Schiller asked me to write a prologue, I, who am not a defender of the guerrilla, merely a poor prophet of what was going to happen and what did happen. At that time, she was very young, and I was a man in my forties; I had already been part of fervent debates among young Latin Americans who saw armed insurrection as the only way of ending an unjust and corrupt society. If Margrit Schiller had been in Buenos Aires at the end of the 1960s, she might have engaged in debate with me and, on hearing my arguments, might have denounced me as a bourgeois reactionary, as the young Peronist Montoneros came to label me in those years. Not because I supported the military regimes or the corrupt politicians elected by the people in those times, but because those young people longing for change knew me as a leftist revolutionary, but that at the same time I was trying to convince them that the guerrilla option would end in total failure, in the loss of the best people, that it would give the forces of reaction an opportunity to strengthen their exploitative and corrupt society on a yet more solid base—as did happen, sadly.

Everything began in Havana in 1960, barely a year after the Cuban Revolution of January 1959, when a small group of Argentinians, including myself, had a meeting with Che Guevara. At that meeting he tried to convince us that the way of changing the Argentinian regime was through a guerrilla war, which should begin in the mountains around Córdoba, in the center of Argentina. I remembered that, countering his argument, I pointed out that the forces of repression in Argentina were much better organized than those of Batista's Cuba, and I listed one by one all the state organizations that existed to combat any leftist rebellion. Che looked at me with an expression of profound sadness and uttered just four words in response to my long arguments with regard to the forces of repression: "They are all mercenaries." I recall that after a moment of silence, the other Argentinians broke into applause.

At that moment, I understood everything, and that reply enabled me to understand what happened afterward. I said to myself, "Clearly to be a revolutionary you cannot begin by analyzing the obstacles, but you have to believe in your own convictions and throw yourself into fighting injustice through rebellion, that gift of the gods for those who believe in altruism and solidarity." But I could not do that, because of the way I am, and when Che's ideas became reality in the streets of Argentina, I continued to warn that death and reversal would be the outcome. Yet at the same time as I was issuing these warnings my understanding and my solidarity with the persecuted grew.

Margrit Schiller is one of those protagonists in other latitudes, in the First World, where it is much more difficult to understand her actions than if she had been in the Third World. But I am not one of those who would confine myself to calling the group which she joined, the Red Army Faction, or Baader-Meinhof, a "terrorist" organization, because one would have to explain why it was "terrorist," why it became "terrorist," and to do that you have to understand the history and the context. One cannot speak of the RAF without telling the whole story.

I was a student in Hamburg between 1952 and 1956, and in those years I was a member of the Socialist German Student Union (the Sozialistischer Deutscher Studentenbund, SDS), which leaned toward social democracy. What were those students like barely a decade after Nazism and the most destructive war in history? They wanted to do something. While primary and secondary school children studied German history up to 1913, young people began to ask about more recent history. I remember that the young people in the SDS did not buy the line about the "collective guilt of the German people." They did not recoil from their responsibility, nor did they accept the position: "We are all guilty, and we must ask forgiveness of the Jews and fight the communists." It was the Cold War. The SDS and its young members wanted to understand the role of the powerful in 1933: German industrial capital, the Church, the political parties of the right, from the Catholic Zentrumspartei to the Liberal Party. They wanted to know why the concentration camp executioners were put on trial, while those who gave the orders from behind a desk were able to pursue a new political career, like Prime Minister Kiesinger, President Lübke, the first Baden-Württemberg president, Hans Filbinger, with his dreadful past as a Nazi military judge, or President Carstens, who had been Goebbels's secretary.

There was talk of freedom and democracy and the West, while, at the same time, European countries continued to have colonies and participated in the repression of the peoples, for example, the French in Vietnam and Algeria; later the German social democratic government sold arms to Videla's military dictatorship in Argentina.

I remember the debates that had just begun in those years, and which took off in the late 1960s and early 1970s, when people held strong positions. I remember the search for alternatives to the unjust system and the dream of a socialism free of Stalinism.

There was a kind of double game being played in West German public life: the individual was being taught to be a protagonist, not to follow the example of previous generations that had let themselves be led by a demagogue. They had to learn to defend themselves against unwarranted interference in their lives by the state, not to let themselves be deceived again. For that reason, they were told, they must exercise their autonomy (this was important later, because a section of German youth took this seriously). But at the same time, they were to believe in the United States, in the alliance against evil, which came from the East. That is, they must be protagonists, but within the system.

On reaching adulthood, Margrit Schiller's generation was carried away by a chain of events that was unstoppable: the 1968 student revolution and the beautiful slogan of "all power to the imagination." Then there was the assassination of the student Benno Ohnesorg on a West Berlin street; Jean-Paul Sartre at the head of the German students' demonstrations, declaring that the communists could not bring about the revolution, because they were frightened of it; the shooting of Rudi Dutschke, perhaps the most distinguished of all the 1968 student leaders—an attack that eventually killed him. I remember a poem by Biermann, the great German poet:

Three bullets hit Rudi Dutschke
A bloody attack
We saw it
And we saw clearly who shot him
Oh, Germany, your murderers

Students and peoples of the world also had to confront the struggle of the Vietnamese people against imperialism in that era, and another poem by the German poet Erich Fried refers to the bombs of the guerrilla not those of the US planes:

Vietnam is Germany
Her destiny is our destiny
The bombs for her liberty
Are the bombs for our liberty

Fried was one of the most popular poets of the 1968 generation. War was declared on the capitalist press, among them the Springer Corporation. There was the Prague Spring as another challenge to authoritarianism. Meanwhile, Mao became the guiding light of the Third World, and, in Latin America, with its epic hero Che Guevara so recently assassinated, the whole continent was rocked by protest and insurrection, women joining the vanguard and raising the flag of feminism.

This was the world in which one section of German youth would take such a dramatic stand. The moment came when one had to make a decision: step aside and wait to see what would happen or confront the violence from above with the wounded violence of the oppressed. In Germany, Che would have taken the second path.

How were German youth supposed to react—young people who had been taught to lead the struggle for the rights of all—when they discovered that US bombers were taking off from German territory on their way to obliterate Vietnamese people and even perversely to poison their forests with Agent Orange? That is what drove the Red Army Faction to bomb US military bases—because it was there, on the military airfield of Frankfurt, that the US planes landed with their cargo of incendiary bombs on their way to kill the Vietnamese people. Why did Germany and the rest of the democratic world not shout out loud: "What is the United States doing in Vietnam?"

What were they supposed to do, these young Germans

who were expected to demonstrate civic courage following Auschwitz? Their options were: stand up in the Bannmeile (where one was permitted to demonstrate no closer than three hundred meters from the Bundestag), knowing that in parliament there was total silence on this subject, pray, distribute leaflets, or vote every four years for another politician who would remain silent—or say, as was said in Argentina: "No violence." I have heard so many politicians and priests say: I am against all violence. We are all against violence, but … And? It exists—and how am I supposed to react to violence? To say no to violence but accept in silence that at that moment a US bomber kills in silence 163 children in a Vietnamese school?

I do not have the answer. Margrit Schiller did have an answer. She lost, and all of us who did nothing or at the most signed a petition or went on hunger strike for three days, we said, "You made a mistake"—just like all the right-wing, centrist, and leftist opportunists, the silent masses who spend their summer holidays at the beach, the young people who are training to be the best managers, the political representatives and the mayors, the priests and vicars, the lecturers and teachers, and the high intellectuals of the left. Margrit was mistaken, but she did not repent. We were not wrong, but we lost as much or more than her. This book about the armed struggle enables us to learn about Margrit's honest mistakes and to see ourselves in the mirror. Margrit Schiller, with her truth and honesty. The cynics and cynicism, the greatest of all corruptions, congratulated with tears after doing their duty as great democrats, applauded, appearing on television, receiving awards. Our democrats. We look at ourselves in the mirror and we see ourselves in them. And in the statistics of starvation. Despite Stammheim. Despite solitary confinement.

Margrit Schiller, thank you for your life, and for your book.

APPENDIX

The Surprising Success of the Red Army Faction: A Brief Chronicle by André Moncourt and J. Smith

On April 3, 1968, four young revolutionaries set fire to two department stores in the city of Frankfurt, in the Federal Republic of Germany. This act of political arson, protesting the FRG's complicity in the ongoing imperialist massacre in Vietnam, is often cited as a precursor to what would become the Red Army Faction.

Within forty-eight hours, Horst Söhnlein, Thorwald Proll, Gudrun Ensslin, and Andreas Baader were arrested and charged with arson. They remained incarcerated throughout their trial but, following sentencing, were temporarily released on appeal in the summer of 1969. When their appeal was turned down, Baader and Ensslin went underground, having decided to pursue the course of armed struggle in a more ambitious and organized manner. What this meant, in practical terms, was finding others who shared their views, engaging in political discussions, learning new skills, and developing an underground infrastructure (safehouses, weapons, etc.).

Andreas Baader was captured in West Berlin on April 3, 1970, set up by an undercover police agent. As an early example of an orientation that would predominate for much of the decade, securing his liberation became a priority for those left on the outside.

A plan was hatched by several women from the nascent armed struggle scene, including well-known journalist

Ulrike Meinhof. Out of fear that the men guarding Baader would not take an all-woman commando seriously, and that this would force them to resort to violence, a male comrade was also integrated into the operation. As we have recounted elsewhere:

> A plan was hatched, whereby Meinhof would use her press credentials to apply for permission to work with Baader on a book about youth centers, an area in which by now they both had some experience. The prison authorities reluctantly agreed, and on May 14 Baader was escorted under guard to meet her at the Institute for Social Issues Library in the West Berlin suburbs.
>
> This provided the necessary opportunity. Once Baader and Meinhof were in the library, two young women entered the building: Irene Goergens, a teenager who Meinhof had recruited from her work with reform school kids, and Ingrid Schubert, a radical doctor from the West Berlin scene. They were followed by a masked and armed Gudrun Ensslin, and an armed man. Drawing their weapons, these rescuers moved to free Baader. When an elderly librarian, Georg Linke, attempted to intervene, he was shot in his liver. The guards drew their weapons and opened fire, missing everyone, and all six jumped out of the library window and into the getaway car waiting on the street below.
>
> Barely a month after his arrest, Baader was once again free.[1]

The process of building infrastructure and finding allies continued, despite ongoing arrests. At the same time, new people were also finding their way to the guerrilla, including many who had been active in the vibrant West Berlin antiauthoritarian scene and several who had been around the Socialist Patients' Collective in Heidelberg. Most of those captured in this initial period could only be charged under Paragraph 129 (membership in an illegal organization) or with minor crimes; after serving their relatively short sentences, many of them would rejoin the guerrilla.

The ability of the Red Army Faction to attract new members, even as it sustained regular losses, is what stands out, not only in this period but for much of the next sixteen years. Indeed, not only attracting new members, but putting forth analyses, interpretations, and strategic visions while doing so. It was as the aforementioned arrests were ongoing that Meinhof and others were working on "The Urban Guerrilla Concept," as detailed in Margrit Schiller's memoir. This text established the RAF not only as a group with a practice but also as a group with a purpose and a plan, attempting to look beyond the scenes its members came from, to grapple with the forces and legacies and limits of the broader society within which they found themselves, and to recognize their historical context and what it made necessary.

In May 1972, just over one year after the release of "The Urban Guerrilla Concept," the RAF went into action.

The May Offensive, as it would come to be known, consisted of a series of bombings. Targets included police stations and US army headquarters, to protest killer cops and the ongoing war in Vietnam. Four American soldiers were killed, and dozens of other people, including civilians, were injured. As RAF member Brigitte Mohnhaupt would later explain, "This decision, this project, was arrived at through collective discussions involving everyone in the RAF; in other words, there was a consensus of all the groups, of the units in each of the cities, and everyone clearly understood what this meant, what the purpose of these attacks was."[2] Years later, individuals involved would recount with pride how they had been told that posters celebrating the bombings had gone up in Vietnam and how the computer damaged in one of the attacks had been used to plan bombing sorties.

There followed a wave of repression, as police, supported by both West German and US intelligence units, set up checkpoints and carried out raids across the country. Within a few weeks Andreas Baader, Jan Raspe, Holger Meins, Gudrun Ensslin, and Ulrike Meinhof—those whom the state would accuse of being the group's "ringleaders"—were all in custody, along with several other RAF members.

Some journalists point to the wave of arrests in June and July 1972 as the end of a putative "first generation" of the RAF—a convenient but untenable view, as many of those who had been captured by this point would upon their release return to the underground, playing important roles in the group's practice not only later in the 1970s but in the 1980s as well. Indeed, some supporters would dismiss the term *generation* as an invention of state and counterinsurgency forces meant to suggest that successive waves of combatants were in fact members of different organizations, part of an ongoing strategy to divide the prisoners and break solidarity.

Unbeknown to most people, some RAF members survived the 1972 crackdown and set about the long task of recovering and reorganizing the project in new conditions. This would come to involve three former RAF prisoners—Margrit Schiller, Helmut Pohl, and Ilse Stachiowak—who hoped to lay the basis for an underground armed initiative to free the prisoners. This, however, never got very far, and most of those involved would become known as the "4.2 Group," following their arrest on February 4, 1974. As Schiller recounts in this volume, "At the time, the highest sentence for membership in a criminal organization was five years. Because the court was unable to prove that we had done anything specific and the Office of the Federal Prosecutor had no political interest in making the details of our activity public, we all received prison sentences of between four and five years, which were relatively short in comparison to others. Only Christa [Eckes] would be sentenced to longer, because of the bank robbery. I got four years and three months."[3]

Beyond the persistence of members from the group's earliest days, two important factors contributing to the RAF's longevity were heavy-handed state repression and the resistance of the RAF political prisoners. On September 13, 1974, Ulrike Meinhof announced the beginning of the group's third collective hunger strike, demanding an end to the brutal isolation conditions. After almost two months, on November 9, Holger Meins died of a combination of starvation and brutal force-feeding, but the strike would continue until outside supporters had been moved to reconstitute the group, issuing a communiqué on February 2, 1975, ordering the prisoners to resume eating. "We are taking this weapon away from you," they explained, "because the prisoners' struggle—given the existing balance of power—is now something that we must settle with our weapons."[4]

What this meant became clear in short order: on April 25, 1975, a RAF commando seized the top floor of the West German embassy in Stockholm, Sweden, taking twelve hostages and demanding the release of twenty-six West German political prisoners. When Swedish police failed to heed warnings to back off, the FRG's military attaché Lieutenant Colonel Baron Andreas von Mirbach was shot. A special intervention team was flown in from Hamburg, telephone lines to the embassy were cut, and the surrounding area was evacuated. Slightly more than one hour later, with negotiations going nowhere, the commando shot dead the FRG's economic attaché Heinz Hillegaart.

Shortly before midnight, as police were preparing to storm the building, the explosives the guerrilla had laid detonated. The state and media would claim that the explosives went off due to some error on the part of the commando; the guerrilla would suggest that the police intentionally triggered the explosion. One RAF member, Ulrich Wessel, was killed on the spot. Police rushed in, and five RAF members were captured. Despite the fact that he had a fractured skull and burns over most of his body, Siegfried Hausner was only hospitalized for a few days. Then, over objections from doctors in Sweden and Germany, he was flown to Stammheim prison, where he died soon after.

The state had attempted to capitalize on its initial capture of the guerrilla, only to find that from within prison they had managed to inspire their successors. Chancellor Helmut Schmidt went so far as to claim that "anarchist guerrillas" now posed the greatest threat the Federal Republic had encountered during its twenty-six-year history. Destroying the prisoners, or at least undercutting their support, became a top priority.

Political prisoners had been subjected to harsh isolation for several years by this point. Prison conditions were intended to break the victims, either to bring them to such a point as that they would be willing to publicly denounce their comrades or, alternately, to drive them mad or incapacitate them. Different prisoners coped in different ways, but in all cases the treatment amounted to torture. At one extreme was the "Dead Wing" or "Silent Wing"—sections of prisons emptied of all or almost all other prisoners, leaving a political prisoner alone with their thoughts, sometimes combined with various forms of sensory deprivation.

The use of isolation and sensory deprivation had been studied by doctors in Canada and the United States since the late 1950s, that line of research being taken up in the FRG by Dr. Jan Gross of Hamburg's Eppendorf University Hospital. Studies carried out by Gross found that sensory deprivation consistently caused feelings of unease ranging from fear to panic attacks, which could progress to an inability to concentrate, problems of perception (including hallucinations), vegetative disorders, including feelings of intense hunger, chest pains, disequilibrium, trouble sleeping, trembling, and even convulsions. Almost half a century later, the harm inflicted by isolation is well-documented, while the practice has metastasized to ever-more obscene dimensions, tens of thousands of prisoners being subjected to various forms of isolation on any given day, the vast majority of them in the United States.

Isolation was a devastating weapon used to attack the prisoners, but it was not the only one. When Ulrike Meinhof maintained her political principles even after months of extreme isolation, a new ploy was attempted. On the basis of an operation she had undergone in 1962 to correct a swollen blood vessel in her brain, Federal Prosecutor Peter Zeis theorized that her political behavior might be the result of some neurological problem. Zeis reached out to Dr. Hermann Witter of the University of Homburg-Saar's Institute for Forensic Medicine to have tests conducted—using restraints and anesthesia if necessary—with the ultimate goal of mandating neurosurgery, regardless of Meinhof's wishes. "It would be so embarrassing," Zeis mused at the time, "if it turned out that all the people began to follow a mad woman." International public protest, including many doctors, forced the government to drop its plan.[5]

Meinhof had been singled out for special attention ever since the Baader liberation action. As recounted by Katharina Karcher:

[S]ince the armed intruders were not yet identified, [public attention] focused on the only known participant in the attack: Ulrike Meinhof. Shortly after the liberation of Andreas Baader, the chief public prosecutor authorized a nationwide search with a reward of 10,000 deutschmarks (DM) for information leading to the arrest of Meinhof—the first instance of such a reward being offered in Germany since WW II ...

Unlike Baader's arson in 1968, Meinhof's role in his rescue in 1970 required explanation, at least in the eyes of many journalists. Most articles presented Meinhof as a radical leftist author-activist. Some reports, however, attacked her on a more personal level. A *Bild* article, for instance, claimed that Meinhof's personality changed due to brain surgery in 1962. The author noted that "Ulrike—who had always been intelligent but highly nervous and very erratic—was afterward often absentminded. In addition to her clumsy choice of dress, she began to look unkempt." Not only did the journalist pathologize Meinhof, he also depicted her as an unpredictable woman who let herself go after her divorce. In addition, this article and several other reports depoliticized Meinhof's participation in the attack by suggesting that she had acted out of love for her "fiancé" Baader.[6]

This targeting went so far as to allege that Meinhof had committed suicide in 1972 due to differences within the group. While Meinhof may have been singled out for special treatment, all women in the RAF during the 1970s were pathologized by both police and media, often in highly sexist terms.

It was in this context, as well as in the context of the trial of her and the other alleged RAF "ringleaders" at Stammheim, that the state announced on May 8, 1976, that Ulrike Meinhof had been found dead in her prison cell, having allegedly committed suicide. This was almost universally disbelieved, and most on the left took it for granted that she had been assassinated. In Meinhof's own words, part of the court record the day before she was found dead, "It is, of course, a police tactic in counterinsurgency conflicts, in guerrilla warfare, to take out the leaders."[7] Her sister, Wienke Zitzlaff, similarly rejected the possibility of suicide: "My sister once told me very clearly she never would commit suicide," she remembered. "She said if it ever were reported that she killed herself then I would know she had been murdered."[8]

Meinhof's apparent murder, combined with the ongoing isolation torture of the other political prisoners, was to push those on the outside to make a second attempt to pressure the state to release the prisoners. A series of hunger strikes and attacks in 1977—including the assassination of Attorney General Siegfried Buback, held responsible for the prison conditions, a failed rocket attack against his successor's offices, and a failed kidnapping, in which banker Jürgen Ponto was killed—culminated in the September 5, 1977, kidnapping of Hanns Martin Schleyer, probably the most powerful businessman in Germany at the time.

Schleyer was president of both the Federal Association of German Industrialists and the Federal Association of German Employers and had a reputation of being an aggressive opponent of any and all workers' demands. He had joined the SS in 1933, just two months after his eighteenth birthday, and had held several important positions in the National Socialist German Students' Association before and during the war. In 1943, he began working for the Central Federation of Industry for Bohemia and Moravia, where he was in charge of "Germanizing" the economy of Czechoslovakia. Following the Nazi defeat, he was captured by French forces and imprisoned for three years, classified as a "fellow traveler" by the denazification authorities. He was released in 1949 and used his experience during the Nazi occupation of Czechoslovakia to get hired to the foreign trade desk in the Baden-Baden Chamber of Commerce and Industry. There cannot have been a more fitting example of everything that was horrible in West Germany, not only in the eyes of the RAF but in the view of the left and the "sixties generation" more broadly.

Within a day of Schleyer's kidnapping, the commando demanded the release of eleven political prisoners, includ-

ing Gudrun Ensslin, Jan Raspe, and Andreas Baader, and
their safe passage to a country of their choice. Despite the
prisoners' assurances that they would not return to West
Germany or participate in future armed actions if exiled, on
September 6, the state declared that they would not release
the prisoners under any circumstances. That same day, a
total Contact Ban was instituted, depriving all political prisoners of any contact with each other or the outside world. All
visits, including those of lawyers and family members, were
forbidden. The prisoners were also denied all access to mail,
newspapers, magazines, television, and radio:

> While the Contact Ban was initially not sanctioned by
> law, parliament obliged by rushing through the appro-
> priate legislation in record time (just three days) and
> with only four votes against. The justification offered
> was a claim that the prisoners had directed the kid-
> napping from within their cells with the help of the
> lawyers. As evidence, police claimed to have found a
> hand drawn map used in the kidnapping in [attorney]
> Armin Newerla's car on September 5.[9]

There ensued a series of ultimatums from the guerrilla
insisting that the prisoners be freed or else Schleyer would
be killed. Meanwhile, all of West Germany was placed under
de facto martial law, and several lawyers who had defended
the RAF prisoners were arrested.

On October 13, with negotiations deadlocked, a Palestinian commando intervened in solidarity with the RAF, bringing the already intense confrontation to an entirely different
level. The four-person Commando Martyr Halimeh, led by
Zohair Youssef Akache of Waddi Haddad's PFLP (External
Operations), hijacked a Lufthansa airliner travelling from
Majorca, Spain, to Frankfurt, in West Germany—ninety people on board were taken hostage.

The airliner was first diverted to Rome to refuel and to issue the commando's demands. These were the release of the eleven RAF prisoners and two Palestinians being held in Turkey.

The plane flew to Cyprus, and from there to the Gulf, where it landed first in Bahrain, then in Dubai, followed by South Yemen. On October 16, it departed for Mogadishu, Somalia, arriving in the early hours of October 17. The dead body of Flight Captain Jürgen Schumann, who had apparently sent out coded messages about the situation on board, was pushed out the door. At 11:00 p.m. that day, sixty members of the GSG-9, West Germany's "antiterrorist" special forces unit, stormed the airliner; guerrilla fighters Zohair Youssef Akache, Hind Alameh, and Nabil Harb were killed, and Souhaila Andrawes was gravely wounded. All hostages were rescued unharmed, with the exception of one man who suffered a heart attack.

The next morning, October 18, at 7:00 a.m., a government spokesperson publicly announced the resolution of the hijacking. An hour later, another spokesperson announced the "suicides" of Gudrun Ensslin and Andreas Baader and the "attempted suicides" of Jan Raspe and Irmgard Möller. Raspe subsequently died of his injuries.

As with Meinhof in 1976, the 1977 Stammheim deaths were widely viewed as murders.

Baader and Raspe died as a result of gunshot wounds, Ensslin as a result of hanging, and the sole survivor, Irmgard Möller, suffered multiple stab wounds.

As to the obvious question of how prisoners could have acquired guns, a prison spokesperson suggested that it was "not out of the question ... that one of the prisoners' lawyers passed the contraband articles to a prisoner during a visit." This despite the fact that before entering the visiting area, lawyers had to empty their pockets and give their jackets to an employee for verification, and they were body searched physically and with a metal detector. Prisoners were strip searched and inspected and given a new set of clothes both when entering and leaving visits with lawyers. Furthermore, due to the Contact Ban, the lawyers had been unable to see their clients after September 6.

Andreas Baader is supposed to have shot himself in the base of the neck in such a way that the bullet exited his fore-head. Repeated tests indicated that it is virtually impossible for an individual to position a gun against his or her own body in such a way. Equally curious, there were three bullet holes in the cell: one lodged in the wall, one in the mattress, and the third, the cause of death, lodged in the floor. Baader had powder burns from the recoil on his right hand, despite the fact that he was left-handed. In the case of Raspe, no powder burns were found.

The gun smuggling theory relied very heavily on the testimony of Hans Joachim Dellwo, brother of RAF prisoner Karl-Heinz Dellwo, and Volker Speitel, the husband of RAF member Angelika Speitel. They had both been arrested on October 2, 1977, and charged under Paragraph 129 with belonging to a criminal association. Under police pressure, both men would admit to acting as couriers for the guerrilla and testify that they were aware of lawyers smuggling items to the prisoners during the Stammheim trial, which had ended in April 1977—they eventually specifically claimed that guns had been smuggled in. The scenario put forth by the state was that these guns were then hidden away in the walls of the cells when renovation work was done on the seventh floor the previous summer. Both men received reduced sentences and new identities in exchange for their testimony.

As well as conveniently explaining the deaths, the gun smuggling story served two further purposes. From that point on, all lawyers' visits with RAF prisoners were conducted through a screen, a process which facilitated auditory surveillance, as well as depriving the prisoners of one of their last direct human contacts. Furthermore, the guards were also permitted to look through lawyers' files "to prevent smuggling."

In the case of Gudrun Ensslin's "suicide," there were further contradictions. The chair she allegedly used to hang herself was too far away to have been used and the cable supporting her would not likely have tolerated the weight of a falling body. As had been the case with Ulrike Meinhof, forensic tests that would have established if Ensslin was dead before she was hanged were never conducted.

Making the state's story even more unbelievable was the fact that not all of the prisoners had died.

On October 27, Irmgard Möller, the only survivor from the alleged group suicide attempt, had her lawyer issue a statement that she had *not* attempted suicide. She said that the last thing she heard before going to sleep on the night in question was two muffled bangs. She was not aware of anything until she awoke some hours later feeling intoxicated and disoriented and having difficulty concentrating. She had been stabbed repeatedly in the chest, the blade penetrating down to her heart sac. The state later claimed that she had done this to herself, using a prison-issue butter knife she had squirreled away. She has always denied this claim.[10]

As a macabre postscript to all of this, RAF prisoner Ingrid Schubert, who was being held in isolation in Munich-Stadelheim prison, was found hanged dead on November 11, 1977. On the Thursday before her death, she had assured her lawyer that she had no intention of committing suicide.

Following the events of 1977, although the Contact Ban was officially lifted, RAF prisoners remained subject to heightened isolation measures. At the same time, a vast manhunt was underway on the outside. There were a number of arrests over the next year, and several RAF members were killed: Willy-Peter Stoll was slain by police while eating in a Düsseldorf restaurant, Michael Knoll was shot dead in an exchange of fire when RAF members were surprised by police during target practice in a wooded area, Elisabeth von Dyck was gunned down without having a chance to surrender on her way to a safehouse in Nuremberg, and Rolf Heißler was shot in the head (he miraculously survived) while entering a safehouse in Frankfurt. As RAF member Rolf-Clemens Wagner would remark decades later, "In the aftermath [of 1977], taking as few additional prisoners as possible became the line. At the end of the seventies, three comrades who were on the wanted posters were shot in the head .... At the time, we called it the 'killer manhunt.'"[11]

It is important to note that hundreds of supporters were also arrested during these years, for "crimes" like passing out leaflets about prison conditions, painting pro-RAF graffiti, or making public statements in support of the guerrilla. This repression was almost always carried out using Paragraph 129 (and its various amended versions, 129a, 129b, etc., each with broader scope and harsher penalties than the last). Paragraph 129 was also used against those who engaged in more militant actions, as the burden of proof was much easier to meet; for instance, the "dpa occupiers," who on November 6, 1978, forced their way into the offices of the Deutsche Presse-Agentur news agency in Frankfurt, cutting the telephone lines and tying up the staff, hoping to send out a press statement about RAF prisoners Karl-Heinz Dellwo and Werner Hoppe, who were on hunger strike and in grave health.[12] The eleven occupiers would each receive one year in prison under Paragraph 129; several of them would end up in the same prison as Margrit Schiller and Verena Becker.

Nonetheless, the RAF persisted. On June 25, 1979, the group carried out its first attack since the Schleyer kidnapping, and its first action in seven years that was not aimed at securing the prisoners' release: the attempted assassination of NATO Supreme Allied Commander Alexander Haig, in Belgium. Plastic explosives were planted by the road that Haig normally took to work, and as his car passed by the charge was manually detonated; however, something went awry, for the general sped off, and it was soon apparent that he had escaped uninjured. The commando would later explain: "Our error was in thinking that we could manually trigger the explosion precisely enough with the target moving that quickly."[13]

As would become clear, the RAF had reoriented its attacks away from prisoners' issues, taking aim instead at targets related to the military-industrial complex, most specifically NATO. This would create an opening for rapprochement with a new generation of young radicals, as a vigorous anti-war movement developed in the FRG in the 1980s, in opposition to plans to deploy short-range US nuclear missiles in the country. At the same time, almost a decade after the Eckhofstraße squat in Hamburg, a shared milestone of several who had subsequently joined the RAF, a new squatting movement of unprecedented proportions was taking root, providing a base for supporters who coalesced into what became known as the anti-imperialist (or "anti-imp") scene.

The early 1980s were a time of reorientation and crisis, and not just for the RAF. The 2nd of June Movement, a guerrilla group initially based in West Berlin and often juxtaposed to the RAF in popular and scholarly accounts, had been decimated by arrests and found itself incapable of renewing its forces. In 1981, the two remaining members on the outside released a statement declaring that they were dissolving their organization and joining the RAF. At the same time, many RAF members were disillusioned and burnt out, a situation that was resolved with the help of a contact one of the new 2JM recruits had established with the East German Stasi, which provided false identities and new lives to a number of guerrillas who sought to leave the struggle.

That same year, the RAF prisoners engaged in another collective hunger strike, joined this time by hundreds of other prisoners. Sigurd Debus, a political prisoner from an independent guerrilla group active in the Hamburg area in the early 1970s, died of a cerebral hemorrhage during one of the brutal force-feeding sessions. As would become standard, this prisoners' struggle was accompanied by vigorous solidarity actions on the outside:

> The following days witnessed dozens of bomb threats across the country, accompanied by dozens of actual firebomb attacks on government buildings. The Saarbrücken offices of the Ministry of the Interior were hit, as was the Lübeck Employment Office, and the Psychology Institute at Hamburg University. The Max Planck Institute's West Berlin offices were also bombed, a communiqué explaining that the institute was being targeted for its research into torture, and antinuclear activists blew up a power mast at a nuclear power plant near Bremen, drawing a clear connection to the hunger strike in their communiqué. At the same time, over a thousand people marched in Hamburg with banners that read "We Mourn Sigurd Debus," and various SPD offices were firebombed in the port city.[14]

Later that year, the RAF carried out two attacks, both aimed at NATO targets. On August 31, a commando detonated a car bomb at Ramstein USAREUR, a US military airbase and the headquarters for NATO air forces in central Europe. While nobody was killed, twenty people were injured. Two weeks later, on September 15, the RAF attempted to assassinate General Frederick Kroesen, supreme commander of the US Army and of NATO's Central Europe Section, firing at his car with an RPG-7 grenade launcher.

These attacks were followed, in 1982, by the release of a new RAF strategy document, "The Guerilla, the Resistance, and the Anti-Imperialist Front." The May Paper or the Front Paper, as it became known, confirmed and explained the significant reorientation of the RAF following the events of the German Autumn. Besides addressing the guerrilla's failed actions in 1977, the document optimistically appraised the potential for revolutionary change in the FRG, described Western Europe as a cornerstone of the worldwide revolutionary process, and suggested an important role could be played by supporters who were not themselves part of the RAF, as part of a broader "front."

The May Paper received a mixed reception from supporters and prisoners, some of whom felt the RAF was revising the key tenets of its historic approach and exaggerating the potential for revolutionary change in the First World, as well as potentially blurring the line between supporters (already liable to be criminalized under Paragraph 129) and guerrillas. Nonetheless, it was clearly necessary to review the previous decade's experiences and their heavy toll and attempt to draw conclusions about how to proceed. Some kind of plan was needed, and that is what the May Paper attempted to provide.

The guerrillas who had been involved in drafting the paper, however, would suffer an unprecedented defeat before it could be fully implemented.

On July 2, 1984, a RAF member in a safehouse in Frankfurt accidentally discharged a weapon while cleaning it, drawing the attention of a neighbor. The police were called, and when they arrived six RAF members were captured. Although it was not known at the time, this was the entirety of the RAF, every single guerrilla who had been active in the previous years was now in custody.

It is testimony to the particular context that existed, in no small part thanks to the May Paper, that the July 1984 arrests did not constitute a death blow. The RAF had proposed a plan in which it had specifically indicated the importance of other allied forces in Western Europe and singled out the role that could be played by supporters, "the resistance." What's more, the two years following the May Paper's release had been spent, not carrying out bombings, but engaging in conversations and base building. As such, the RAF was uniquely well-placed to overcome what should normally have ended the project, as new members stepped into the breach.

In December 1984, prisoners initiated a new hunger strike. The statement announcing their strike enumerated the various forms of abuse they had been subjected to over the years, as well as articulating the central position that NATO now held within the RAF's strategic view, very much in line with the May Paper: "During the reconstruction phase that followed the US system's defeat in Vietnam, NATO was fascistically restructured as a strategic military alliance to support US policies at home and abroad. In this situation, their survival depends on keeping the West European metropole under control."[15]

On December 18, the RAF went into action, targeting NATO's SHAPE officers' training school in Oberammergau. A car bomb was left in the school's parking lot—however, security guards identified and successfully defused it. The RAF claimed the attempted bombing in a phone call to the media the next day.

The bombing may have been a technical failure, but it nonetheless acted as a signal, unleashing a wave of attacks across the FRG. Siemens's Frankfurt offices had already been firebombed on the night of December 16. This was followed by attacks against the Camp Lindsey US Air Force compound in Wiesbaden, the US Military Intelligence Detachment in Düsseldorf, the US Army Radio Station antenna in Edigen near Heidelberg, a data center in Reutlingen, and many more. On December 31, the French Technical Arms Mission in Bonn was bombed, as was the British Army's Rhine-Main barracks in Osnabruck, the Bundeswehr Officers' Academy in Hamburg, and the NATO pipeline in Hohenahr. All in all, seventy-one arson and bomb attacks and countless spraypainting actions would be recorded in the course of the hunger strike.

While some journalists reported these as "RAF attacks," in actual fact they were the work of anti-imps—the "anti-imperialist resistance"—operating within the scope of the front, as had been suggested in the May Paper. As the militants who bombed AEG-Kabelwerke in Mülheim explained: "The step taken by the comrades in prison is a signal for the resistance in the FRG. The demand as it is now formulated and the struggle to achieve it transcends the old dividing lines, and itself constitutes the practice necessary for a common perspective of the guerrilla and the anti-imperialist resistance." In their words: "The guerrilla is the core of this vision, because as a result of its practice and its options, acting on the terrain of armed illegality, it embodies the conflict between imperialism and revolution."[16]

Unlike RAF attacks, attacks carried out by the resistance (or the Fighting Units [Kämpfenden Einheiten], a common name adopted by some groups) did not aim to inflict human casualties; despite the use of bombs, the goal was consistently limited property destruction. The only person who died during this wave of bombings was a young supporter, Johannes Thimme, who was killed when the bomb he and a comrade were transporting prematurely exploded.

The front had a second dimension, beyond that of coordination between the guerrilla and the aboveground resistance. It also implied collaboration with other guerrilla groups elsewhere in Western Europe that had similarly adopted a focus on anti-NATO attacks, especially the French group Action Directe and the Italian Red Brigades.

Action Directe issued a joint statement with the RAF during the hunger strike, and then, on January 25, assassinated General René Audran, a high-level official in the French Ministry of Defense. Just days later, on February 1, a RAF commando assassinated Ernst Zimmermann, president of the Federation of German Aviation, Space and Equipment Industry (BDLI) and CEO of the MUT arms corporation.

The 1984–1985 winter offensive marked a high point for the RAF. Never before had such a wide range of radical militants and organizations collaborated to support the guerrilla. The strategy outlined in the May Paper seemed to be working.

That said, just as military defeat, the capture of the guerrilla in July 1984, had been mitigated by political preparation, the successes of the winter were to be largely undone by a subsequent political blunder.

On August 8, the RAF bombed the Rhein-Main airbase, the most important American military base in Europe. Although attacks had never stopped after the 1984–1985 hunger strike, the Rhein-Main bombing launched a new offensive, by some measures even greater than that which had accompanied the winter hunger strike. But this was at best a pyrrhic victory, for at the same time as the Fighting Units and other illegal militants were launching their attacks, controversy around how the airbase bombing had been carried out would eat away at the guerrilla's support in ways that later appeared decisive.

RAF members had abducted a young GI, Edward Pimental, who was drinking at a bar, in order to use his ID to get on to the base. Once they had what they needed, they killed him. To many, including numerous supporters and a number of prisoners from the RAF, this was an act of needless brutality, targeting not one of the architects of imperialist policy but, instead, one of its least powerful instruments, a young soldier. The fact that the guerrilla did not seem to understand what the problem was, and that even when they issued a self-criticism they insisted on dismissing many critics as "arseholes on the left," did not help matters.[17]

Indeed, more than a few RAF prisoners were aghast. Irmgard Möller recalls: "When we heard about the letter ... in which they claimed it, we first thought that it was a fake. We in the Lübeck prison shouted to each other through the windows: 'It's a counteraction.' When it became clear that it wasn't an intelligence agency action, we couldn't initially make sense of the fact."[18]

For some of the political prisoners, the "unnecessary" death of a soldier would constitute a nodal point, where quantitative changes gave way to a qualitative shift. According to Karl-Heinz Dellwo, "When the young American soldier Edward Pimental was shot, simply to get his duty pass, I—and this is true of other RAF prisoners as well—publicly distanced myself for the first time."[19]

It would be almost a year before the RAF acted next, in July 1986. Using two propane canisters loaded with explosives and detonated by remote control, the Mara Cagol Commando assassinated Karl Heinz Beckurts, the chairman of the Federal Union of German Industry's Atomic Energy Working Group and Siemens director for research and technology, also killing his driver. This was followed in October by the assassination of Foreign Department Director Gerold von Braunmühl, a career diplomat who was publicly perceived as having liberal, or even progressive, views.

The Beckurts and von Braunmühl assassinations would signal a new approach: for the next several years, the RAF's attacks would be targeted assassinations of high-level but not particularly infamous government or industry leaders. The fact that these figures were generally not the focus of broad public campaigns made it much more difficult for the state security services to provide adequate protection, as it was largely unclear who the guerrilla might target next. At the same time, it was not always obvious, even to those on the left, how these killings related to any specific political campaigns or movements or why these targets had been singled out.

Imperialism is a complex and massive machine with countless people committed to defending and extending it. In that sense, these assassinations were anti-imperialist—and, indeed, the guerrilla would issue communiqués explaining its choice of target and the role they played in geopolitical developments. Yet fewer and fewer people could follow the thread from one attack to the next. Assassinating politicians or businessmen who most people had never heard of did not constitute a viable or sustainable long-term approach; in fact, the entire project seemed to be spinning its wheels. The late 1980s were not an inspiring time, and the front that had seemed so promising in 1985 and 1986 would eventually become a distant memory. (A process encouraged by a series of arrests in August 1986; with the exception of RAF member Eva Haule, all of the arrested were aboveground supporters.)

On September 20, 1988, Secretary of State for the Minister of Finance Hans Tietmeyer survived a RAF attack when the commando's automatic pistol jammed; on November 30, 1989, Deutsche Bank Chairman Alfred Herrhausen was assassinated in Bad Homburg; on July 27, 1990, State Secretary of the Minister of Interior Affairs Hans Neusel survived an attempted assassination; on April 1, 1991, Karsten Rohwedder, the Chairman of the Treuhandstalt, the organization responsible for privatizing industry in the former East Germany, was assassinated.

The prisoners continued to struggle against their conditions, and, in 1989, engaged in their tenth collective hunger strike for association, to be able to receive uncensored political reading materials and for the release of several prisoners with serious health problems. While the strike failed to win its demands, it succeeded in making connections that had

long eluded the prisoners, gaining support from more liberal quarters, including some politicians in the Green Party
that had emerged earlier that decade. Years later, former
prisoner Helmut Pohl would explain that a message had
been quietly sent to the guerrilla at the same time, asking
it to desist from further attacks in order to create political
space for a broader discussion about the changing political
context, as well as for the prisoners' ongoing need for association and release.[20]

No RAF combatants were captured during this period,
yet the guerrilla was unable to recreate the sense of enthusi-
asm and connection that had existed previously. The group
had first emerged and offered a way forward at a time when
the New Left was in a period of crisis. It had brought in
new members later in the 1970s through the urgency of the
prisoners' own struggles. In the first half of the 1980s, it had
re-rooted itself in new movements that had emerged around
nuclear power, nuclear missiles, and squatting. But, by the
end of the decade, these movements were both declining and
being institutionalized, and the prisoners had no desire to
repeat the failed experiences of the 1970s. What was about to
happen would exacerbate the disarray in ways that nobody
saw coming.

On November 9, 1989, the Berlin Wall came down; this
completely unexpected development would change the
course of world history, and in West Germany it constituted
a tsunami, destroying and washing away most of the reference points and perspectives that had dominated politics up
to then. Within a year, the Germany Democratic Republic
would cease to exist, being legally absorbed into a newly
expanded Germany. Amidst the elation in the streets, more
than a few worried about what a new German nationalism
would mean.

At the same time, this had very practical (if surprising)
consequences for the RAF prisoners: during a two-week

period in June 1990, all of those who ten years earlier had opted for a retirement in East Germany were arrested. To varying degrees, they all cooperated with German prosecutors, often even against their former comrades. As a result of their testimony, new charges were filed, and five prisoners found themselves facing additional prison sentences.

The RAF faced a dire situation on multiple levels: an increasingly demoralized base; a gaggle of turncoats from its past making headlines; the German state emerging from the Cold War triumphant in ways never imagined; the parallel rise of the far right, with increasing attacks on refugees and people of color; the Iraq War clearly spelling out what the New World Order portended for the people of the Global South.

At the same time, imperialism in these years took advantage of its political windfall by resolving contradictions that had festered under the weight of the East–West standoff. This took different forms around the world, but in Germany one of the matters to be addressed was the stubborn refusal of the guerrilla to disappear, despite the numerous blows it had endured.

On January 6, 1991, the government proposed the gradual release of some of the prisoners. By September 1993, eight prisoners from the RAF and its support movement had been released. At the same time, most RAF prisoners remained incarcerated, the Kinkel Initiative (named after Federal Minister of Justice Klaus Kinkel) promising much more than it ended up delivering.

On April 10, 1992, the RAF issued a unilateral ceasefire statement, explaining that no more attacks targeting people would be carried out, with the goal of creating space both for a broad discussion about the changed political situation and for the prisoners to be granted association and, eventually, to be released. "Now it is a question of how the state reacts," they explained. "And because right now nobody knows how they will react, we intend to continue the process of discussion and reconstruction. If they use their repressive extermination machinery to wipe out anyone who is part of this process—i.e., if they continue the war—then, for us, the phase of de-escalation will end—we will not stand by, idly watching without reacting."[21]

While many pundits would suggest that the ceasefire statement was a response to the Kinkel Initiative, the fact of the matter is that it was the culmination of a discussion that had been going on for years, within the guerrilla, with the prisoners, and with the support scene. It was immediately applauded by the prisoners, Irmgard Möller released a statement five days later in which she affirmed "the decision made by our comrades is the correct one, identifying a political process that we prisoners are also part of."[22] The April Statement was followed several months later by the August Paper, in which the RAF pronounced the end of the front concept and called for a broad-based discussion to determine the next step to be taken by the movement.

Terms like de-escalation and ceasefire conjure up a sense of relaxation, of lessened tension. In reality, nothing could be further from the truth. Like going faster when running downhill, it is easy to escalate—it is when you try to quickly slow down that you are most likely to trip and fall. The period the RAF had entered would prove to be one of its most perilous, as the connection between political and military developments played out to the guerrilla's disadvantage.

On March 27, 1993, the RAF carried out its next—and final—attack. Weiterstadt prison had taken eight years to build and cost 250 million marks (approximately $155 million). It was supposed to be a state-of-the-art prison, a high-security dungeon that would hold people awaiting deportation, among others. A RAF commando scaled the fence around the construction site, tied up the security guards, and then laid explosives. The blast did over $80 million in damages and delayed the prison's opening by four years. There were no casualties. "Given that a year had passed and the state had still not responded to the statement announcing the cease-fire, the RAF wanted to demonstrate that it continued to pose a threat but without escalating things," Birgit Hogefeld would later explain.[23]

One month after the Weiterstadt bombing, an infiltrator in the anti-imp scene, Klaus Steinmetz, managed to lure Hogefeld and her fellow RAF member Wolfgang Grams to a meeting in the town of Bad Kleinen. It was a trap, with GSG-9 agents deployed to swoop in, hoping to capture the entire guerrilla if possible. Hogefeld was immobilized right away, but Grams managed to make a run for it, with agents in hot pursuit. He shot and killed one, before being subdued. According to eyewitnesses, as he lay prone on the tracks, agents shot him multiple times, including once at close range in the head. He died several hours later at the Lübeck university hospital.

For the first time in the RAF's existence, an informant had managed to get close enough to the guerrilla to set them up for capture and execution. A period of intense soul-searching was inevitable, not only in the Wiesbaden scene (where Steinmetz had been active and vouched-for for years) but for the guerrilla as well. In addition to this, the tensions inherent both in de-escalation and the lure of the Kinkel Initiative, as well as disagreements among the prisoners (exacerbated by solitary and small-group isolation), brought things to a head. In October, RAF prisoners Christian Klar, Brigitte Mohnhaupt, and Eva Haule each issued statements announcing a split, accusing the RAF and certain prisoners of negotiating with the state, using de-escalation and armed struggle as bargaining chips for the release of prisoners.

There followed a series of statements and counterstatements by prisoners and by the RAF, staking out positions and making and denying accusations. At issue were conversations Green Party politician and lawyer Christian Ströbele had had with business and government representatives in the hopes of securing the prisoners' release in the new context of the ceasefire. The guerrilla denied engaging in negotiations, but the unavoidably ambiguous way in which its statements counterposed the ceasefire with warnings that it might resume heavier actions if the state attacked the prisoners left space for different interpretations. The Weiterstadt action itself—an attack on a prison, normally something everyone should be happy about—was criticized as being part of a new "populist" approach in which armed activity was used to curry favor and exert pressure, i.e., as a bargaining chip. The polemics were public but difficult to appraise, unless one was directly involved.

One final document would be issued by the RAF during this period, in March 1994. "On Steinmetz, the April Statement, and 'Social Counterforce'" provided a sober summation of the experiences of the previous several years and an important analysis of the errors that had led to Bad Kleinen.[24]

The RAF would issue three short statements in 1996 addressing claims made in the media and attempts by state security forces to criminalize an alleged supporter but would never carry out another action. The assumption was that the group had simply disbanded, but then, in April 1998, a final statement was mailed to Reuters news agency:

> Almost 28 years ago, on May 14, 1970, the RAF was born in an act of liberation. Today we are ending this project. The urban guerilla in the form of the RAF is now history.

> We, that is, all of us who were part of the RAF at the end, are taking this step collectively. From now on, we, like all others who come out of this context, are former RAF militants.

We stand by our history. The RAF was the revolutionary attempt by a minority to resist the way things were developing in this society and to contribute to the overthrow of capitalist conditions. We are proud to have been part of this effort.

The end of this project indicates that we were not able to succeed in this way. However, it does not speak against the necessity and legitimacy of revolt. The RAF represented our decision to stand on the side of those who were struggling against the ruling class and for worldwide liberation. For us, it was the right decision.[25]

In this final document the RAF attempted to sum up its history, examining the past decades of struggle, even as the authors acknowledged that they themselves had only joined the organization very late in its development. Specifically regarding 1993, they explained that "in the end, the extremely painful split between a section of the prisoners and ourselves, in which we were declared enemies, persuaded us that the conditions that had given rise to the RAF—solidarity and the struggle for collectivity—had completely disappeared."

At the time that the RAF announced it was no more, nine RAF prisoners remained incarcerated. The last of these, Birgit Hogefeld, would not be released until June 2011.

According to police, several former RAF members remain at large. On July 20, 1999, in Duisburg, an armored car was attacked with a rocket launcher and robbed of an estimated one million DM. The state contended that DNA evidence tied three former RAF members to the robbery. Many years later, in 2016, the state would claim that the three had been involved in numerous subsequent robberies, including two other attempted rocket-launcher attacks on armored vans in 2015.[26]

Former RAF prisoners have been subject to repeated attempts at recriminalization, and the state has occasionally resuscitated investigations, even though people had already been convicted and spent years incarcerated for the attacks in question—the excuse being to find out "who really did it." Certain turncoats, chief among them Peter-Jürgen Boock, have been instrumental in this process. In one extreme case, in 2011, Christa Eckes was threatened with "coercive detention" when she refused to testify against Verena Becker. It had been almost twenty years since Eckes had been released from prison, and at the time she was undergoing chemotherapy in a final battle against cancer. It was only following protests in a number of cities in Germany and elsewhere in Europe that the state backed down, with the Federal Court of Justice in Karlsruhe ruling that due to her health any period of incarceration would put her life at risk.[27]

"The RAF was never the path to liberation," the guerrilla would explain in their final document, but "it was perhaps one aspect of it." It may surprise some that we refer to the success of the Red Army Faction, but, measured by the experiments of its day, it remains one of the groups that managed to renew itself, to speak to succeeding generations of people, and to have a major influence on the society in which it found itself. Even though only a very small minority agreed with its message, and its own membership would vary between single- and double-digits, it had a far greater impact than much more popular and populous organizations.

The RAF was central to a process whereby a significant amount of space was created for militant resistance in Germany, and political antagonism enjoyed a greatly extended half-life. While it would be mechanistic to claim that it had initiated this process, the RAF was one aspect of a dialectic that generated useful possibilities and perspectives that are unlikely to have occurred otherwise. This is not to say that this political space was occupied solely by those who agreed with the RAF's actions or analysis, but the fact that a small number of people were willing to think outside the box, to do what nobody else felt was realistic, to make demands not based on what they thought they might win but on what they felt was necessary, and that they stood by their decisions even at great personal cost, helped to produce a fertile political terrain on which others could build. And, indeed, the RAF became an inspiration not only within Germany but elsewhere as well, both in Western Europe and in North America.

Former RAF members have been candid about their views of their own experiences, and especially of their errors. While this is a valuable contribution, it is not an unambiguous one, as there is no consensus among those who spent time with the RAF. Different people have different opinions, not only about why things happened and how they should have happened but also about what happened. This extends even so far as the Stammheim deaths, with some former prisoners claiming that they do believe the prisoners committed suicide (albeit under extreme duress), while others remain certain that this was a state execution.

While the broader context—political, cultural, and technological—has been deeply transformed since the RAF was active, there remains much to be gleaned from this history and from the guerrilla's own words about their experiences. This text provides only a very schematic history of this legacy of resistance, more work remains to be done to recover these experiences and to make them accessible to English-speaking comrades.

Appendix Endnotes

Unless otherwise noted, all websites accessed December 5, 2020.

1 André Moncourt and J. Smith, *The Red Army Faction: A Documentary History of the Red Army Faction, Volume 1: Projectiles for the People* (Oakland: PM Press/Kersplebedeb, 2009), 54.

2 "Brigitte Mohnhaupt, Gefangene aus der RAF in Stammheim am 22.7.76," Social History Portal, https://socialhistoryportal.org/sites/default/files/raf/0019760722_01_5.pdf; available in English as "The Structure of the RAF (Mohnhaupt and Pohl at Stammheim Trial)," German Guerilla, http://germanguerilla.com/1976/07.

3 Cf. 162.

4 "Letter from the RAF to the RAF Prisoners," in Moncourt and Smith, *The Red Army Faction*, vol. 1, 338.

5 Moncourt and Smith, *The Red Army Faction*, vol. 1, 241.

6 Katharina Karcher, *Sisters in Arms: Militant Feminisms in the Federal Republic of Germany since 1968* (New York: Berghahn, 2017), 47–48.

7 "Journalists Unearth Rare Terrorism Trial Tapes from 1970s," *Deutsche Welle*, July 31, 2007, https://tinyurl.com/y4j8bdmb.

8 United Press International, "Urban Guerilla Leader Hangs Herself in Cell," *Hayward Daily Review*, May 10, 1976.

9 Moncourt and Smith, *The Red Army Faction*, vol. 1, 479.

10 Ibid., 514–17.

11 Rüdiger Göbel, Peter Rau, Wera Richter, and Gerd Schumann, "Wir wollten den revolutionären Prozeß weitertreiben" (interview with Helmut Pohl and Rolf Clemens Wagner), *junge Welt*, October 17,

2007, https://www.jungewelt.de/beilage/art/263580; available in English as "We Wanted to Push the Revolutionary Process Forward," German Guerilla, https://tinyurl.com/jz5hcdy.

12 André Moncourt and J. Smith, *The Red Army Faction: A Documentary History, Volume 2: Dancing with Imperialism* (Oakland: PM Press/Kersplebedeb, 2013), 96–97.

13 Ibid., 116.

14 Ibid., 160.

15 "Hungerstreikerklärung," *Zusammen Kampfen* no. 1 (December 1984): 5, Social History Portal, https://socialhistoryportal.org/sites/default/files/raf/0019841200_0.pdf; available in English as "Hunger Strike Statement," German Guerilla, http://germanguerilla.com/1984/12/01/hungerstrike-statement.

16 "Kommunique," in *Widerstand heisst Angriff!! Erklärungen, Redebeiträge, Flugblätter und Briefe* (Amsterdam: Bibliotheek voor Ontspannungen en Ontwikkeling, 1988), 163, https://socialhistoryportal.org/sites/default/files/raf/0019880000_0.pdf.

17 "An die, die mit uns kampfen," January 1986, *Zusammen Kämpfen* 5 (January 1986), Social History Portal, https://socialhistoryportal.org/sites/default/files/raf/0019860100_01_2.pdf; available in English as "To Those Who Struggle Alongside Us," German Guerilla, http://germanguerilla.com/1986/01.

18 Alexander Strassner, *Die dritte Generation der "Roten Armee Fraktion"* (Wiesbaden: Westdeutecher Verlag, 2003), 147 (translation, Moncourt and Smith).

19 Michael Sontheimer, "Wir mussten verlieren" (interview with Karl-Heinz Dellwo), *Spiegel*, October 11, 2007, https://www.bellastoria.de/publications/interviews/wir-mu%C3%9Ften-verlieren (translation Moncourt and Smith).

20 "Wir müssen jetzt Wege zur Entlassung finden" (interview with Helmut Pohl), *Angehörigen Infor* 182 (June 15, 1996), Social History Portal, https://socialhistoryportal.org/sites/default/files/raf/0019960600_0.pdf; available in English as "Interview with

Political Prisoner Helmut Pohl on the Politics of the Red Army Faction (RAF)," German Guerilla, https://tinyurl.com/y5q9ehvz.

21 "An Alle die auf der suche nach Wegen sind wie menschenwürdiges Leben hier und weltweit an Ganz konkreten Fragen organisieret und durchgesetzt warden kann," *Interim* April 1992, Social History Portal, https://socialhistoryportal.org/sites/default/files/raf/0019920410_01_2.pdf; available in English as "Who Are Searching for a Way to Organize and to Create a Dignified and Life Worthy of Human Beings, Here and Around the World, by Addressing Concrete Issues," German Guerilla, http://germanguerilla.com/1992/04/10/to-all-who-are-looking.

22 Irmgard Möller, "Erklärung der Gefangenen aus RAF und Widerstand," *Interim*, May 1992, Social History Portal, https://socialhistoryportal.org/raf/6101; available in English as "Statement by Irmgard Möller Regarding the RAF Cease-Fire," German Guerilla, https://tinyurl.com/yyaqal8c.

23 Gerd Rosenkrantz, "Wir waren sehr deutsch" (interview with Birgit Hogefeld), *Spiegel*, October 13, 1997, https://www.spiegel.de/spiegel/print/d-8799444.html (translation Moncourt and Smith).

24 "Erklärung zu der vergangenen Phase (zu Steinmetz etc)," Social History Portal, https://socialhistoryportal.org/sites/default/files/raf/0019940306_0.pdf.

25 "Die Auflösungserklärung der RAF vom März 1998," Social History Portal, https://socialhistoryportal.org/sites/default/files/raf/0019980300_2.pdf; available in English as "'The Urban Guerrilla Is History': The Final Communiqué from the Red Army Faction (RAF)," German Guerilla, http://germanguerilla.com/1998/03.

26 Kate Connolly, "Former Red Army Faction Members Linked to Botched Robbery," *Guardian*, January 19, 2016, https://www.theguardian.com/world/2016/jan/19/former-red-army-faction-members-linked-to-botched-robbery.

27 "Christa Eckes—Honor Her Memory!" German Guerilla, June 20, 2012, http://germanguerilla.com/2012/06/20/christa-eckes-honor-her-memory.

About the Authors

Margrit Schiller was a member of the Red Army Faction in the early 1970s, and as a result spent most of that decade in West German prisons. Released in 1979, she moved to Cuba in 1985, and then to Uruguay in 1993. After ten years in Montevideo, she returned in Germany. She now lives in Berlin. She has described her experiences in Cuba and Uruguay in her memoir *So siehst du gar nicht aus! Eine autobiografische Erzählung über Exil in Kuba und Uruguay* (Assoziation A, 2011).

Ann Hansen served seven years of a life sentence in Canadian federal prisons for acts carried out as part of the group Direct Action. She is a prison abolition activist and author of *Direct Action: Memoirs of an Urban Guerrilla* (Between the Lines, 2001) and *Taking the Rap: Women Doing Time for Society's Crimes* (Between the Lines, 2018).

Osvaldo Bayer (1927–2018) was an author, journalist, and scriptwriter who was exiled from Argentina during the years of military dictatorship. His works include *The Anarchist Expropriators: Buenaventura Durruti and Argentina's Working-Class Robin Hoods* (AK Press, 2016), *Anarchism & Violence: Severino Di Giovanni in Argentina 1923–1931* (Elephant Editions, 1985), and *Rebellion in Patagonia* (AK Press, 2016).

André Moncourt and **J. Smith** are the coeditors of *The Red Army Faction: A Documentary History, Volume 1: Projectiles for the People* (Kersplebedeb and PM Press, 2009) and *Volume 2: Dancing with Imperialism* (Kersplebedeb and PM Press, 2013), with a third and final volume forthcoming.

KER
SPL
EBE
DEB

Since 1998 Kersplebedeb has been an important source of radical literature and agit prop materials.

The project has a non-exclusive focus on anti-patriarchal and anti-imperialist politics, framed within an anticapitalist perspective. A special priority is given to writings regarding armed struggle in the metropole, the continuing struggles of political prisoners and prisoners of war, and the political economy of imperialism.

The Kersplebedeb website presents historical and contemporary writings by revolutionary thinkers from the anarchist and communist traditions.

Kersplebedeb can be contacted at:

Kersplebedeb
CP 63560
CCCP Van Horne
Montreal, Quebec
Canada
H3W 3H8

email: info@kersplebedeb.com
web: www.kersplebedeb.com
        www.leftwingbooks.net

Kersplebedeb

ABOUT PM PRESS

PM Press is an independent, radical publisher of books and media to educate, entertain, and inspire. Founded in 2007 by a small group of people with decades of publishing, media, and organizing experience, PM Press amplifies the voices of radical authors, artists, and activists. Our aim is to deliver bold political ideas and vital stories to all walks of life and arm the dreamers to demand the impossible. We have sold millions of copies of our books, most often one at a time, face to face. We're old enough to know what we're doing and young enough to know what's at stake. Join us to create a better world.

PM Press
PO Box 23912
Oakland, CA 94623
www.pmpress.org

PM Press in Europe
europe@pmpress.org
www.pmpress.org.uk